7/99

NINE INCH NAILS

St. Martin's Griffin ❧ New York

NINE INCH NAILS: SELF-DESTRUCT

BY MARTIN HUXLEY

Photo of Trent Reznor on title page courtesy of Neal Preston, Retna Ltd., © A&M Records

Design by Bryanna Millis

Library of Congress Cataloging-in-Publication Data

Huxley, Martin.
    Nine inch nails / by Martin Huxley.
        p.   cm.
    ISBN 0-312-15612-X
        1. Nine Inch Nails (Musical group)   2. Reznor, Trent.   3. Rock
    musicians—United States—Biography.   I. Title.
    ML421.N56H89   1997
    782.42166'092'2—dc21
[B]   97-5105
                                                               CIP
                                                                MN

First St. Martin's Griffin Edition: July 1997

10   9   8   7   6   5   4   3

The author wishes to thank the following individuals for their contributions and support in the making of this book: Jim Fitzgerald, Regan Good, Tara Schimming, Madeleine Morel, Holly George-Warren, Shawn Dahl, Michael Krugman, Paddy Cohen, Tara Key, Tim Harris, Dave & Regina Dunton, Drew & Meryl Wheeler, Kelly Keller, Michael Ackerman, Christopher Sobczak, Ira Robbins and Leslie Morgan.

CONTENTS

NINE INCH NAILS

INTRODUCTION

Nine Inch Nails represents perhaps the most unlikely success story in contemporary popular culture, having bludgeoned the mainstream into submission with a distinctly individual brand of music that's as uncompromising as it is personal. Combining the aggression of heavy metal, the tribal rhythms of dance music, the unyielding clatter of industrial rock and unflinchingly lurid lyrics that confront alienation, obsession, twisted sex, torture, self-destruction, rage and despair, Nine Inch Nails takes the dance-noise style of such pioneering "industrial" groups as Cabaret Voltaire, Ministry and Skinny Puppy to its logical extreme. Meanwhile, leader and sole charter member Trent Reznor's visual appearance and lyrical attitude, which originally echoed that of such dark-hued goth bands as Bauhaus and Sisters of Mercy, quickly took on a distinctive identity that owed nothing to the goths and everything to Reznor's own tortured psyche.

While none of the aforementioned goth acts ever transcended cult status, Nine Inch Nails has conquered a broad fan base by balancing Reznor's bleak worldview with sonic catharsis that echoes the primal release offered by heavy metal. As Reznor has said, "I can make something loud, but how can I make it the loudest, noisiest, most abrasive thing I've ever heard? Can I go ten steps past the goriest horror film you've ever seen in a way that's more disturbing than cheesy? I know I can; I've done it. If you're not ready for it, it's terrible, it's noise. On a couple listenings, if you get that far, you hear through the distractions and find a beauty under the surface ugliness." **3**

Nine Inch Nails's violent, venomous music represents the uncompromised vision of its darkly charismatic vocalist, songwriter, multi-instrumentalist and sonic architect. Reznor, the band's uncontested leader, has described his motivations thusly: "I'm not afraid to think about certain things you aren't supposed to think about. I mean, I do wonder what it would be like to kill somebody, though I'm not going to do it. But I know why people idolize serial killers."

Since the release of Nine Inch Nails's 1989 debut album *Pretty Hate Machine*, through the subsequent multi-platinum efforts *Broken* and *The Downward Spiral*, Reznor has emerged as one of the most compelling figures of the nineties alternative-rock explosion, a black-clad antihero whose impassioned diatribes against conventional mores have established him as a beloved icon of rage and despondency. Reznor is also an obsessive perfectionist whose artistic zeal and personal intensity are equalled by his marketing savvy, as well as a multimedia visionary who has extended his unsettling musical vision with a series of unforgettably gruesome videos (some of them so strong that they've never been officially shown to the public) and in an overpowering, multisensoral stage show. In short, Reznor has managed to maintain and broaden his outsider's perspective, even as he's subversively penetrated the pop charts. Or, as *Rolling Stone* put it, "As an ultimate antihero, Reznor stands as far outside the mainstream of American popular culture as it may be possible for a million-selling rock singer to get."

"I think Nine Inch Nails is big enough and mainstream enough to gently lead people into the back room a little bit, maybe show them some things it might have taken them a little longer to stumble into on their own," Reznor told *Rolling Stone*. "That back room could represent anything that an individual might consider taboo yet intriguing, anything we're conditioned to abhor. Why do you look at an accident when you drive past, secretly hoping that you see some gore? I shamefully admit it—I do."

In short, the complex, contradictory Reznor makes a fascinatingly unlikely pop star, one who freely admits to being deeply uncomfortable with the trappings of stardom—and one who, despite his ambivalence about the position of cultural influence he's found himself in, embraces the opportunity to bring his extreme yet oddly accessible music to mainstream ears.

"Nine Inch Nails deals with the addictive part of my personality," Reznor told *Spin*. "How many mushrooms can you take? What happens then? What about mushrooms *and* DMT? Nine Inch Nails offers me the chance to do what I want to do. I want a show, a spectacle. I'm allowed to look stupid. And I want to."

CHAPTER 1

"Maybe my obsessive desire to find extremes has to do with growing up where nothing ever happened," Trent Reznor would later say, and the details of his early life would seem to bear this out.

Michael Trent Reznor was born at 7:30 on the morning of May 17, 1965 in Mercer, Pennsylvania, a rural farming town (population approximately 2,500) in the state's northwest corner. Mike Reznor—who had worked as a commercial artist and interior designer as well as being an amateur bluegrass musician—had married Nancy Clark while both were still in their teens, not long before Trent's birth. Since there was already one Michael in the family, their son was always called by his middle name. Trent's parents split up shortly after his sister Tera, his only sibling, was born in 1971. After that, Trent—who as a child suffered from allergies to cats, dust, grass and ragweed—lived mainly with his maternal grandparents, while Tera stayed with Nancy, who lived nearby.

Like many children of his generation—including his fellow future alternative-rock icons Kurt Cobain and Eddie Vedder—Trent was the product of a broken home, offering much ammunition to those who would subsequently attempt to peg the anger and loneliness in his later work as a reflection of his separation from his parents. Reznor has generally downplayed the issue, though he admits, "I know I haven't come to terms with all that shit. I just felt sort of . . . off to the side."

As he would tell *Alternative Press* in 1990, "My grandparents are good people and good parents, but I feel like anybody does whose parents split up—kind of ripped off. I'm not going to make it out to be some big fucking kind of deal. Subconsciously, it may have some kind of effect, but it didn't seem to be that bad. You just realize you're not on *Happy Days*. It's the real world; you need to ignore what you are programmed by sitcoms to think your life should be. I don't really think about it and I don't put any blame on anybody. My parents were young. I would have done the same thing, I'm sure."

Despite his parents' breakup—and despite his subsequent image as an avatar of alienation—by most accounts Trent had a happy and healthy boyhood. Though he has since painted himself as a childhood outcast, not everyone remembers it that way. "He was always a good kid," his grandfather Bill Clark told *People* magazine in 1995, remembering Trent as a Boy Scout who enjoyed fishing, skateboarding and building model planes. And music.

"Music was his life," said Clark, "from the time he was a wee boy. He was so gifted."

In addition to studying saxophone and trumpet, Trent showed serious potential as a classical piano prodigy, and was encouraged by his family to pursue his nascent talent. "It came really naturally to me," he would later recall in an interview with *Spin*. "Knowing that I was good at something played an important role in my confidence. I was always shy, uncomfortable around people. I slipped by. But with music, I didn't."

Those who knew Trent as a teenager describe him

as clean cut and popular. He played tenor sax in the Mercer Junior and Senior High jazz and marching bands. "I considered him to be very upbeat and friendly," recalled Mercer band director Hendley Hoge. "I think all that 'dark avenging angel' stuff is marketing, Trent making a career for himself."

"I hated school . . . I fucking hated it," Reznor claims. "The fact is that it revolved around something you didn't have access to. If you weren't on the football team, if you were in the band, you were a leper. When people say those were the best years of our lives, I want to scream."

Reznor recalls his first childhood role model being Steve Austin, TV's *Six Million Dollar Man*, whose bionic programming enabled him to transcend human frailties. The character appealed to him, he told *Details*, "probably because I wasn't the biggest kid in the class and I wasn't the athletic superstar football player. I always thought he was cool. The day the Bionic Woman died on *The Six Million Dollar Man*, that was a tearful day in our household. When I think back, I had a degree of feeling mildly depressed, of melancholiness." Years later, Trent would regularly use the name Steve Austin as his alias when checking into hotels while on tour.

Despite the built-in cultural limitations of his small-town environs, he recalls being raised in what he described to *Musician* as a "liberating, questioning environment." "My parents allowed me to do things that my friends weren't allowed to do. I smoked pot with my dad the first time. I didn't have to be in by midnight. It was an open environment. And when I moved away I didn't completely fuck myself up or become a drug addict, like some of my friends who had a more oppressive home life."

While he may have spent more time with his grandparents during his formative years, it's obvious that Mike Reznor—who remains an avid Nine Inch Nails supporter—was a major influence on young Trent. "My dad and I are best friends. He's pretty much responsible for the way I turned out," he has said. "He would provide a little artistic inspiration here and there in the form of a guitar, stuff like that."

Still, Trent found life in the cultural backwater of Mercer to be stifling. He would later describe his hometown as "a nice little picturesque one-horse, one-McDonald's kind of town. I go back there now and it's like 'What a nice pleasant place,' but not a place to grow up in.

"My scope of travel was maybe a half-hour radius, and every little town had the same Kmart and Cineplex playing the same five movies, all Sylvester Stallone," he told *Musician*. "It's hard for people who've grown up in cities to understand that, to have an endless cornfield for your backyard. But that's what a lot of America is—it's not dodging gunfire from gangs."

Reznor would later theorize that his subsequent embrace of musical and psychological extremes stems from a "desire to escape from Small Town, U.S.A., to dismiss the boundaries, to explore. My life experience came from watching movies, watching TV and reading books and looking at magazines. And when your fucking culture comes from watching TV every day, you're bombarded with images of things that seem cool, places that seem interesting, people who have jobs and careers and opportunities. None of that happened where I was. You're almost taught to realize it's not for you.

"Growing up, I so wanted to get the fuck out of where I was, away from the mediocrity and mundaneness of rural life," he told *Spin*. "Anything extreme caught my attention. I was intrigued with the limit, the movie that scared the shit out of me, the book—I had a huge collection of scary comic books when I was a kid.

"I remember seeing *The Exorcist* when I was eleven or twelve," he recalls. "It fucked me up permanently because it was the most terrifying thing I could ever imagine. I couldn't discredit it like I could *Alien*. Because I'd been fed all this bullshit by Christianity that said yes, this could happen."

If his musical studies helped boost Trent's confidence, they also served to intensify the budding prodigy's sense of alienation from his peers. "It wasn't cool to play music where I was from. You had to be an athlete," he told *Rolling Stone*. "The teachers in my school were shitty for the most part, and I got a pretty bad education because I had a bad attitude. If I wanted to get good grades, I could. Stuff I'd like to know now, at the time, I thought was irrelevant; typical teenage stupidity."

Despite his shyness, Trent came out of his shell long enough to play prominent roles in his high school's productions of *Jesus Christ Superstar* and *The Music Man*, as Judas and Professor Harold Hill respectively. He was even voted "Best in Drama" by his classmates. But any theatrical aspirations he may have had went up in smoke the first time Trent heard Kiss.

"Kiss changed my world," he would later tell *Spin*. "It seemed evil and scary—the embodiment of rebelliousness when you're age twelve and starting to get hair on your balls."

His discovery of rock music also spelled the end of Trent's career as a classical pianist. "I was encouraged to drop out of school, get tutored, practice for ten hours a day for a concert career," he recalls. "But I'd just discovered Kiss, so that was out of the question. I knew I wasn't going to get laid studying piano with a nun."

Instead, he had other ideas about how to implement his musical training. "My dad got me an electric piano. He had a little music store that sold acoustic instruments in the back room, where me and a couple other guys started jamming in terrible garage bands. I realized that music wasn't all about learning a piece on the piano.

"I started fucking around with guitar, and I was never good at guitar. I'm still not good at it. I took lessons off my dad for a couple of months, and then said 'Look, I'd rather just fuck around on it, and not know.' I still only know two bar chords. But I don't care. The naiveté with which you approach an instrument can lead to exciting results."

While in high school, he says, "I begged my parents

to get me a real cheap Moog. Now I could play (The Cars's) 'Just What I Needed.' "Thus equipped, the former classical prodigy began playing keyboards with a series of local bands.

Unlike many musicians of his age group who lived in more cosmopolitan areas, the teenage Reznor never got the opportunity to experience the liberating influence of punk and other left-of-center musical genres. "You have to understand. I was in a geographical area where by the time I'd hear something it was already dead. There was no college radio. There were no alternative record stores. There was no independent anything. There was no MTV. There was nothing. My world was comic books and science-fiction shit. Scary movies. Whatever I could absorb. And it kind of ingrained in me this idea of escape from Pennsylvania."

As he later told *USA Today*, "I didn't want to accept that my destiny was to pump gas down the street. I don't mean to be condescending. A lot of people are happy in that environment, my family included. My friends stayed, and they're happier than I am. But I wanted out."

CHAPTER 2

After graduating from Mercer High in 1983—just as the still-new MTV was exposing a generation of kids in the American heartland to an array of vaguely exotic-sounding new acts, many of them synthesizer based—Trent made his first concerted effort at breaking out on his own. He enrolled at Allegheny College, a small, relatively conservative liberal-arts school about ninety miles north of Pittsburgh. There, he studied music and computer engineering, and made a concerted—and, he says, mostly unsuccessful—effort to fit in socially.

"No one in my family ever finished school. I thought, okay, in high school I was a fuckin' loser, I didn't fit in. So I thought in college I'm going to make some friends, try to fit in. But I was banished instantly. I felt like a misfit."

By this time, the eighteen-year-old Reznor was working steadily with a local group, Option Thirty, whose repertoire was a combination of new-wavey originals and covers of then-current hits by the first wave of MTV-spawned British stars. "They did U2, Billy Idol, Tears for Fears—all that early MTV stuff," recalls one observer.

Despite his recollections of being a misfit, Reznor did manage to make a few new friends while at Allegheny. Andrea Mulrain, at the time a seventeen-year-old freshman, dated Trent during his college days. "I noticed him within my first few days on campus," she remembers, "just because he looked like an interesting character. He had a different image then—shorter hair, dyed red. He looked like a creative type, so I approached him and asked **19** him if he was from New York, and he said, 'No, I'm from Mercer.'

"The first time I saw him perform with Option Thirty, it was immediately obvious that he had star quality and that he had a very special talent, even though he was doing covers. The next day was my birthday, and he came to my dorm room and brought me a makeshift birthday cake made out of Twinkies.

"I was immediately struck by Trent's personal drive," says Mulrain, who is now an A&R executive for London Records. "Even then, he was one of the most focused and driven people I've ever known. He was a bit shy and reserved, but he was super-confident when it came to his music. When most other guys were joining fraternities and getting into the Allegheny spirit of things, Trent was doing gigs and writing songs and having equipment shipped to his dorm room."

Mulrain recalls Reznor already having a deep affinity for electronic music. "When I met him, he was already tinkering and experimenting with programming, and experimenting a lot with his keyboards. He was one of the first people in America to have a Memory Moog; he ordered it specially from Japan or wherever they make them, and he was very excited about that. Although he was studying computer engineering at Allegheny, he had already taught himself a tremendous amount about programming, and he was very adept at figuring out anything to do with computers or keyboard instruments."

The increased mainstream prominence of machine-generated music in the early 1980s was a revelation for Reznor. "It really was exciting," he said. "Sequencers were just coming out. I was going to college for computer engineering and I thought, 'I love music, I love keyboard instruments—maybe I can get into synthesizer design.' The excitement of hearing a Human League track and thinking, that's all machines, there's no drummer. That was my calling."

Though he has since claimed that he didn't engage seriously songwriting until much later, Andrea Mulrain remembers some early compositional efforts: "He was always writing original stuff, in addition to playing covers. He loved synth-pop, and he was always experimenting with that kind of writing. He hadn't discovered the industrial thing yet, so it wasn't as noisy. It was more melodic and less technological, and I think the subject matter was more traditional and not as pained. It wasn't as intense as what he'd do later. I don't think he'd found that aspect of his songwriting voice yet."

By the end of his first year at Allegheny, Trent had decided to put his academic efforts on the back burner, in order to focus on his musical career. "He knew that he had to make a choice," Mulrain states, "and he realized that he really did need to throw all of his creative energies into the music. We were in a couple of computer science classes together, and as far as I can remember he did quite well, but the music began to overtake the studies.

"Toward the end of that year, he was doing three shows a week, and he was playing in Ohio a lot and traveling back and forth. He changed his schedule so that he was only going to school a couple of days a week, so he could do more shows. He came to a decision toward the end of the year, that he was going to have to make a choice between college and music. So he decided to leave Allegheny and go off and try to get a job in a studio somewhere.

"For all the time I've known him, Trent's never been one to sit around and let life happen around him. He'll go out and if he needs to do twenty different jobs to make his record sound the way he wants it to sound, he'll do whatever it takes. He's totally in control, and he always has been. He always has a clear, focused vision of what he wants, and he'll takes whatever steps are necessary to get that."

Reznor himself presents a more modest assessment of his sense of focus at the time. He told *Spin* that, after leaving college, "I spent a year doing nothing. I lived with my dad out in the woods. And I was playing in cover bands. Three hundred bucks a week. It was the most whorish part of my career so far. I played keyboards and sang. My destiny was lounge bands."

CHAPTER 3

After a period spent spinning his wheels in various forgettable local groups (including an Erie, Pennsylvania-based, new-wave cover outfit known as The Urge), Trent decided to relocate to Cleveland, the better to work on establishing a musical career. While gray, economically depressed, industrial Cleveland wasn't exactly New York or Los Angeles in music industry terms, it was a good deal headier than rural Pennsylvania. Though its music scene had cooled down somewhat since the halcyon days that produced such influential underground bands as Pere Ubu and Rocket from the Tombs, Cleveland still offered considerably more in the way of opportunity than rural Pennsylvania.

"I moved to Cleveland, because the band I was in was playing there a lot," Reznor later explained to *Spin*. "There was a music store that had all the high-tech synthesizers and sequencers that were coming out. I was there all the time. They offered me a job. Ten to six, every day. Hearing twenty people bang on drum machines.

"Cleveland wasn't that bad. It's lacking in some things, but it provided a good place for me to get my shit together."

While working days at the music store, Trent joined a series of local bands. The most embarrassing of these, apparently, was a commercial hard-rock outfit known as The Innocent. Though he didn't play on the group's locally released album—the unironically titled *Living on the Street*—he joined in time to have his picture appear on the cover, with a dated-looking keyboard instrument slung over his shoulder.

In the future this phase of his history would constitute a major skeleton in Reznor's career closet. When confronted on the subject by *Details* writer Chris Heath a decade later, Reznor dismissed the innocent disc as "Foreigner crap . . . dinosaur AOR bullshit rock. . . . Stupid. Dumb," adding, "You got me. I'm an idiot. I've tried to hide it. It was the one thing I was waiting for someone to throw at me."

Not much more memorable, according to witnesses, was Slam Bam Boo, a would-be commercial synth-pop group with whom Reznor performed live and did a bit of recording.

Less humiliating was Trent's tenure as keyboardist with Lucky Pierre, a darkly arty outfit led by Cleveland scene veteran Kevin McMahon, who would reemerge a decade later as the brains behind the one-man band Prick, which would be amongst the first batch of acts signed to Reznor's Nothing label. Reznor played live with Lucky Pierre for a couple of years in the mid-eighties, and later appeared on the group's 1988 EP *Communique*.

Apparently, the most serious of Reznor's pre-NIN bands was Exotic Birds, a progressively inclined combo whose personnel also included drummer Chris Vrenna, an old high-school friend from Mercer who worked with Trent at the music store.

Perennially broke, Reznor and Vrenna shared a squalid apartment in a bad part of town. "Our unit of currency used to be LPs," Trent recalled of that lean period. " 'That shirt costs three LPs and two twelve inches? No way.' Then it became video-game cartridges, back when a forty-dollar gas bill was enough for us to worry about for a week. The currency was drugs for me for a while—that's the ultimate no value for your money. And at a low point, it was Top Ramen noodles and Busch in cans, because Budweiser was too expensive, and Ramen will technically keep you alive. We kept some Old Milwaukee around in case friends came by."

While Exotic Birds's music was undeniably ambitious, it lacked the sonic and emotional edge that Reznor had come to value through his belated exposure to a world of music that hadn't been available to him when he was growing up in Mercer.

"I realized, 'Jesus Christ, there's a lot of music I'd never heard,' " he told *Rolling Stone*. "It was like a musical awakening—from Test Dept. to XTC, all these bands I never knew existed. . . . When I stumbled into all that harder-edged music that incorporated electronic elements—what you, but not I, would call industrial—it pretty much fit in with things that were already in my head. Suddenly, music started to make sense."

Indeed, Trent felt a particular affinity for the first wave of "industrial" bands—so named because their mechanized beats echoed the din of heavy industry. He was particularly drawn to the work of Al Jourgensen, leader of the Chicago-based Ministry and perhaps the most influential figure in the American industrial underground at the time. Like Reznor, Jourgensen began his career playing dance-oriented synth-pop, but eventually modified his approach in favor of a more personal and extreme style.

"What's interesting to me," Reznor stated, "is that Jourgensen has always brought a catchiness to his songs that Einsturzende Neubauten or Test Dept. or Throbbing Gristle, the classic industrial bands, don't. I find a lot of (those bands) unlistenable, (but) Ministry is like fucking good songs arranged in a way that could kick your ass."

While still a member of Exotic Birds, Reznor had a minor brush with mainstream show business, appearing briefly in the Cleveland-shot 1987 Michael J. Fox/Joan Jett movie bomb *Light of Day*, in which he appears briefly as part of a fictitious synth-pop trio called the Problems, which performs a new-wavey reworking of Buddy Holly's "True Love Ways" and is treated as an object of ridicule by the film's equally unconvincing blue-collar rocker characters. Needless to say, the Problems did not appear on the film's soundtrack album.

Exotic Birds did some recording and achieved a moderate degree of recognition on the local scene. But it wasn't long before Trent was finding the group's music to be a bit too polite for his increasingly edgy preferences.

"The bands I was playing in weren't really my taste, in terms of what I would have written, but it was a challenge to step out of what I liked to see if I could play it. I didn't dislike what I was doing, but it wasn't remotely close to what I would have done on my own. I like AC/DC's old records, but I'm not going to play something like that."

Reznor was finding himself less and less interested

in playing other people's music and more inclined to strike out and create something of his own. As he later told *Spin*, "Finally, I was hearing bands that were using electronics, and they didn't sound like Howard Jones or Re-Flex. They had all this fucking aggression and tension that the hardest of heavy metal or punk had. But they were using tools I understood. And it seemed more interesting, because this music couldn't have been made five years ago, let alone twenty. It was based on tools that were *now*."

Trent eventually made the decision to focus his energies and make a serious effort to develop his own music and work to carve out a viable career. "I heard stuff other people were recording and I always thought, 'This stuff sucks.' I thought I could do better, but for a long time I wasn't doing anything about it. I was arranging other people's music. I was playing keyboards on other people's bullshit demos. I was playing live, taking drugs and being a fucking idiot—fooling myself that I was doing something when I really wasn't.

"I hadn't written anything. Ever. I'd never written a song. I was afraid. I always had an excuse not to do it. One day I woke up and said, 'You're twenty-fucking-three years old, what the fuck are you doing? Shit or get off the pot.' So I quit Exotic Birds and got this job doing odds and ends at a studio. And I made a pact with myself. I'd been getting high a lot. I was turning into what I'd never wanted to be. So I started this experiment: What would happen if every ounce of energy went into something? Because I'd never busted my ass."

So he began busting his ass in a major way. He signed

on as an assistant at a local studio, Right Track, where he eventually worked his way up to engineer. Performing menial tasks around the studio gave him the opportunity to hone his recording skills while familiarizing himself with the machinery and computer applications he would need to reproduce the sounds that he was hearing in his head. "I cleaned toilets by day so I could have someplace to work on my music at night," he later told *Request*.

"He was training himself in engineering," recalls one friend, "working at the studio in exchange for studio time. He was pretty studio-friendly already, so he was really just enhancing his knowledge, fine-tuning what he had already learned."

"Here's a guy that would come in and do a session until two in the morning and then start working on his own material until eight A.M.," noted Bart Koster, owner of Right Track. "He is so focused in everything he does. When that guy waxed the floor, it looked great." Koster was so impressed with Reznor's talent and determination that he gave him studio access to work on his own material during off-hours. "How could I possibly stand in this guy's way? It wasn't costing me anything, just a little wear on my tape heads."

"I asked myself," Reznor said in an interview with *Plazm*, " 'What do I want to do? What is my end result?' My end result would be to get myself into a situation where I don't have to worry about a day job, my job can be making music. I'd like to be as successful as I can at that on my terms. How do I get there? Get a record contract. How do I get a record contract? Well, living in Cleveland, every poor fool thinks you go out and play in bars and some idiot's going to see you. It doesn't happen. It doesn't happen there anyway. So I thought, 'Make a tape that's the best I can make.' How do you do that? Well, I didn't have a band, and the only means necessary was electronics."

Having taught himself the MIDI computer applications necessary to sample and refine various sounds, Reznor assembled a distinctive arsenal of noises and rhythms that suited the emotions his songs were exploring, mixing electronics with savage bursts of electric guitar. He later described the process as one of trial and error, "to put something together, think about it, refine it, go back in and do it again. There was a lot of thought put into it. I was trying to get Nine Inch Nails to congeal into a cohesive thing."

Reznor's concern with developing his own music demanded that he become a proficient songwriter with a distinctive lyrical stance. Again, he achieved substantial results through trial and error. After an unsuccessful attempt to write Clash-style political anthems, Reznor looked inward for inspiration. "I needed some kind of input for songs that could have some sort of impact," he says. "I elaborated on what was bugging me."

Reznor's first completed song was the harrowing suicide fantasy "Down In It." "I took a very experimental approach to it," he reports. "The original version I did was about half the speed of the one on the record. And it was a total rip-off of 'Dig It' by Skinny Puppy; I'll admit that now. But, lyrically, I was experimenting with just kind of train-of-thought, writing down whatever I thought.

"After some experimenting and failing on a few different things, I realized that what would make the biggest impression (would be) to make a very honest thing. The only thing I could speak about with any authority was my own personal experience and tried to relate situations I'd been in or feelings I'd thought or dissatisfactions with relationships or religion or the government of the country I live in or whatever it is."

While Reznor's new music drew inspiration from such industrial favorites as Ministry and Skinny Puppy, unlike those bands, his lyrics were unsparingly, viscerally personal and fraught with raw emotion. The results seem to have surprised even him. "It was all stuff out of my journal," he told *Spin*. "This wasn't a character singing lyrics. This was my guts in a song. . . . Now *Pretty Hate Machine* has sold a ton of copies, and I'm dismissed by some as a caricature or a cartoon. But when I wrote this thing, that wasn't a character singing. And I didn't know if I wanted people to know that much about me."

Whatever his misgivings about his songs' emotional nakedness, Reznor spent several months working obsessively on demos, dedicating all of his free time to solitary late-night sessions at Right Track or in his small home studio. The discipline allowed Reznor to immerse himself in the emotional content of the songs he was writing.

As he told *Alternative Press*, he enjoyed the instant grat-
ification of executing his musical ideas without having to
explain those ideas or teach parts to other musicians:
"I've always worked that way, alone. It's pretty normal to
me. If I come up with a cool idea, it's an hour away from
becoming great, an hour of me just fuckin' around, just
doing terrible things until it's developed."

However, he says that, despite the solitary nature of
his Nine Inch Nails debut and his subsequent reputation
as a dictatorial control freak, the one-man-band approach
grew mainly out of necessity. "Every time I ended up asking for help, I ended up disappointed and having to do it
myself."

Additionally, the fact that Reznor was developing
the songs' arrangements with electronics rather than live
musicians played a crucial role in shaping Nine Inch
Nails's sonic aesthetic. "These were the first songs I'd ever
written. And I didn't know what Nine Inch Nails was
about, and when it's one person and a computer, there's
a pretty big palette of sounds and identities you can as-
sume. And it wasn't really based on 'Can I play the guitar,' because I could simulate that through the computer."

While Trent could create the music on his own, he
realized that some help would be required on the business end. Fortunately, John A. Malm Jr., a young veteran
of the Cleveland scene who'd managed several local
bands, had become a Reznor admirer. The two had met
during Trent's tenure with Exotic Birds, when Reznor au-
ditioned as keyboardist for a band that Malm worked

with. He didn't get the gig, but he gave Malm a tape of some of his songs, and the manager was impressed.

"I was dealing with local bands in Cleveland in this kind of sink-or-swim situation; all very learn-as-you-go," Malm recalled. "But when I heard Trent's tape, I thought, 'God, this is the real shit.' "

Just how real would soon become clear.

CHAPTER 4

Reznor emerged from his months of toil and isolation with a polished three-song demo tape that demonstrated how far his artistic vision and his technical abilities had progressed, and how well those two elements complemented each other.

By that time, Reznor had officially adopted the name Nine Inch Nails for his new project. While fans have since come up with all manner of theories to explain the name's significance—that the nails used to crucify Jesus were nine inches long, or that nine-inch nails are used to seal coffins, or that the Statue of Liberty's fingernails are the same length—the real reason, according to an interview Trent did with *Axcess* magazine, is somewhat less colorful.

"I don't know if you've ever tried to think of band names, but usually you think you have a great one and you look at it the next day and it's stupid. I had about two hundred of those. Nine Inch Nails lasted the two week test, looked great in print, and could be abbreviated easily. It really doesn't have any literal meaning. It seemed kind of frightening. It's a curse trying to come up with band names."

Reznor's initial ambitions for his recording career were fairly modest. "At the very beginning, during the summer of '88, we were just going to put a twelve inch out on some European label (and) see what happens. Maybe a year or two later after we get a better idea of what the band is going to be like, we would approach a bigger label. At that time, I didn't know; Nine Inch Nails was three songs. I wasn't sure what direction it was going to go. I didn't want to get involved in a label where it was, 'Hey, that's good, but let's smooth it out here and there, make that pop' or whatever."

But things began to move faster than anyone had anticipated. Trent's demos were impressive enough to elicit positive responses from eight of the ten labels that John Malm, now signed on officially as Trent's manager, approached. "Eventually, we realized that we didn't have to put out a twelve inch on a nothing label. I had my shit together by then."

By the end of 1988, Nine Inch Nails was the subject of serious interest from a number of labels, including Wax Trax! and Nettwerk, the two most prominent labels on the industrial scene and the homes of Ministry and Skinny Puppy, respectively. Meanwhile, Trent had written several new songs and had begun experimenting with live performance, fronting a live NIN lineup that included Chris Vrenna on drums. This embryonic version of the band played a string of ten East Coast shows (some of them as the opening act for Skinny Puppy), including a well-attended Halloween date at New York's Irving Plaza.

It was at the Irving Plaza show that Reznor was approached by TVT Records, a small New York label that had entered the alternative-rock market with mixed success, after having achieved a financial windfall with the company's first release, an album of old TV-show theme songs. TVT's owner and founder was Steve Gottlieb, an enterprising attorney who'd already earned a reputation as both a canny entrepeneur and a mercurial and demanding individual. Gottlieb's label, meanwhile, had already developed a reputation for signing artists to long-term deals.

According to Gottlieb, "The first time I saw Trent live was at twelve noon in an empty club in Cleveland—me, my A&R assistant, a Warner rep who was a friend of the manager, and the manager. Trent and a couple of stand-in people were playing with a tape. He gave a performance which was just chilling, and it was clear that he was not only a musical genius, but a star."

Gottlieb adds, "The original demos (for *Pretty Hate Machine*) were in a very different direction from where the album went. They weren't nearly as dark, and there were a couple of tracks that were kind of house-y. It was (already) great, (but) then he took it to a different level."

Once signed to TVT, the pressure closed in as Reznor's handful of demos had to be fleshed out into a cohesive album. "I kicked into complete work mode," Trent remembered. "It was complete isolation every day. I figured I could round myself out when the record was finished. It weirded me out pretty much. I got to the point where I couldn't be around people. When I was, I was weird and I knew I was weird, but I couldn't help it."

To aid in the construction of Nine Inch Nails's debut album *Pretty Hate Machine*, TVT engaged the services of no less than four prominent producers. Hired for the occasion were John Fryer, whose résumé included work with the Cocteau Twins and Love and Rockets; Flood, who'd worked extensively with Depeche Mode, Erasure and U2; and Tackhead mismasters Adrian Sherwood and Keith

LeBlanc. After beginning work at his home studio in Cleveland, Reznor hooked up with Flood at Boston's Sigma Sound before moving on to London to record the bulk of the album with Fryer.

The big-name quartet of studio pros gave Reznor access to an impressive pool of talent, but the multiproducer approach also created organizational and logistical problems that complicated the album's birth process. It also didn't help that Reznor didn't get along with Fryer. "We had one month in England to do practically the whole album," Reznor told *Spin*, adding that he and Fryer "didn't work on weekends, because he's a 'normal guy.' So by the second week I was dreading weekends. I didn't know one person in England. And I'm not the kind of guy who could ever go to a club in another country by myself. I started getting bummed out, thinking, 'I've got two more days of nothing to do.'"

Reznor later said that he had originally wanted Flood to produce the entire album, but Flood's Depeche Mode commitments didn't allow it. "I liked Flood because he's the opposite of Sherwood. He's very transparent. You don't say, 'Hey, that sounds like Flood' . . . Flood is the type of producer who says, 'Well, I don't care about the status of the band I'm working with. I don't care about money,' which is cool because we didn't have a huge budget to work with."

It was through his association with Flood that Reznor got an early taste of the limelight when he and Flood took some time out from recording to attend a party celebrating the release of Depeche Mode's documentary 101 in New York. "The best thing was standing in the back of the Ritz. There was the singer for Depeche Mode, me, (Mute Records president and Depeche Mode manager) Daniel Miller, Flood and the keyboard player for Depeche Mode. But two kids came up to me, and said, 'Aren't you in Nine Inch Nails? We saw you with Skinny Puppy last year.'

Keith LeBlanc, who first came to prominence playing on influential rap records as the drummer in Sugar Hill Records' house band, was brought in to rework some of Fryer's mixes. "I wasn't into some of the mixing Fryer was into, so I went into the studio with Keith LeBlanc in New York to add yet another studio and sound to the list. Consequently, I had the task of trying to fit that into some sort of cohesive mix of songs, fading them in and out, putting material in between them, which took a long time."

"Working with a bunch of people," Reznor reflected, "was a roundabout, backward way of doing a record. In an ideal situation, if I had musicians who I thought were competent and who I could collaborate with on an equal level, things would be easier. I could write songs faster and it would probably be more exciting. It would be nice to have input from people you respect. When there's somebody you just don't see eye-to-eye with, it's more of a hassle than anything."

While *Pretty Hate Machine* bore the credits of four outside producers, the album would be written, sung, played, arranged and programmed entirely by Reznor, setting the pattern for the recording approach he would successfully employ in the future. "The way I write, there isn't anybody to bounce ideas off of. It's not like a band, where you've got so-and-so on guitar and a bass player and the whole four-piece format. I approached it knowing my tools and my limitations. I'm a shitty guitar player, but that's my style and that's where it's going to be. Same with bass and whatever else. The vocals were one take. I tried to create a very minimal feel."

As he had on his original demos, Reznor relied heavily on samples and programmed rhythm tracks, along with bracing bursts of electric guitar. "*Pretty Hate Machine* was recorded on an old-school Mac, which was about fifteen hundred bucks then, a sequencing program and one sampler that you could buy in the paper for three hundred bucks right now," he told *Plazm*. "A sampler, I think, is the coolest thing, because anything you hear can become anything else. If you want a drum to be a car door slamming, that's what it is. Everyone's got these all-in-one boxes that have every sound in the world in them and it's all preset. They're good arrangement tools, but they're so generic."

Once the album's ten songs had finally been finished, it was Reznor's job to edit the disparate tracks into a complete listening experience. "That was a fuckload of work because I didn't want it to sound like ten songs from ten different producers in ten different countries and studios. Chris Vrenna helped me edit fifteen versions of each song, cutting them together and splicing shit in between the songs so the record flowed."

Reznor has claimed that TVT hated the finished

album. He told *Spin*, "I go back to the States, and the label tells me, 'Hey, by the way, this record is a piece of shit.' "

TVT's reputedly cool response to *Pretty Hate Machine* could be seen as a disturbing omen of things to come. "There was a lot of strain—creative differences, among other things," said Reznor. For instance, he says that he was less than thrilled when Adrian Sherwood's mix of "Down In It" was included on the album by TVT, in place of his own "more emotional, not as linear" version.

Just prior to the album's release, TVT issued a twelve-inch single containing three versions of "Down In It." The single almost immediately struck a responsive chord with the public, reaching the Number One slot on *Rolling Stone's* dance chart and placing in the Top 20 of *Billboard's* Top 20 club chart.

Despite its piecemeal recording process, *Pretty Hate Machine* is a remarkably cohesive work, combining sonic innovation with an absorbingly personal lyrical perspective. "*Pretty Hate Machine* was about juxtaposing human imperfections against very rigid, sterile, cold arrangements," Reznor explained to *Spin*. "You can't just have icy vocals over icy music. If the music is very precise, make a vocal tape that's less perfect, so you've got this meshing of man versus machine."

Indeed, the album's ten songs offered a swirling maelstrom of densely droning electronic noise, violent synthesized beats, edgily impassioned vocals and an unexpectedly accessible melodic sensibility. Meanwhile, Reznor's seethingly personal lyrics railed desperately against a litany of existential frustrations.

Writing in *Thrasher* magazine, journalist Steve Martin described *Pretty Hate Machine* as "the clammy warmth of psychosexual angst set against the detached cold of coarse rhythmic aggression. Nine Inch Nails is an entrancing juxtaposition of imagery and energy built on a foundation of intermingled repulsion and desire."

Alternative Press scribe Jason Pettigrew noted the difference between Reznor and the electro-pop frontmen who had preceded him. "Trent Reznor isn't the kind of guy who moos about having his own personal Jesus or being a victim of love. He does heap on the electronics but he also uses sweat and drums and bold guitars and not one damn tape recorder. Forget all about things gloomy with a touch of mascara; Reznor would rather slap you silly than give you a handkerchief."

The insistently hooky metal-disco anthem "Head Like a Hole" opens the album on an accessibly unsettling note, offering screeching guitar and lyrics deriding bourgeois indulgence. Elsewhere, "Sin," "The Only Time" and "Something I Can Never Have" plumb the depths of personal degradation.

Reznor sets his conceptual sights on considerably bigger game on "Terrible Lie," railing against God Himself. "I believe in God," he told *Spin*. "I was brought up going to Sunday school and church, but it didn't really mean anything. Things upset me a lot. It was just a theme I kept coming back to—religion, guilt and doubting. I believe there's a God but I'm not too sure of his relevance.

"There are just some things that don't seem very fair

in the world, like this fucking hypocrisy of organized religion," he commented to *Alternative Press*. "I just don't understand how people can blindly believe a bunch of the shit they're fed, to believe it so that they don't think too hard about other issues. 'Be a good boy and you'll go to heaven.' If it works for you, fine, but it doesn't work for me and that pisses me off because I kind of wish it did."

Reznor also revealed that "Sanctified," which many interpreted as being about sexual obsession, is actually "about a relationship with a cocaine pipe." "I knew it could be interpreted (as a relationship with a woman), but it was more about addiction." When asked how autobiographical the song was, the singer responded, "Let's just say it was partially fact and partially fiction. The situation has been remedied.

"I don't do many drugs because I can't handle them very well," he further stated. "But I know people that can handle them, as much as you *can* handle drugs."

With his budding popularity came the first wave of media efforts at pegging Reznor's dark musical persona. "These catch phrases like 'mope rock,' 'psychotic techno-pop' or 'angst-ridden' are all bullshit," he grumbled.

"People come up to me like I'm this grim, have-a-noose-around-my-neck-at-all-times kind of person. That's not the case at all," he told *Spin*, while admitting, "I'm not the happiest guy in the world. I'm not sure why. But I can't say, 'It's because someone stole my bike.'

"It's a personal thing. I see a lot of people overanalyzing, asking me if I've had a really tormented sex life, personal life . . . I haven't, not incredibly. I guess I've not always been the happiest person. The last few years have been a little darker than the rest. . . . Not that I'm Mr. Gloom or that I never smile. There's just a side of me that's come out recently, or that I've accepted, that was the main inspiration for these songs. It's what I've found I could express the best."

Even at this early stage, Reznor was resisting the "industrial" tag. "I didn't want to come across as an industrial, snarling, Satan-singing entity. That's not what Nine Inch Nails is. I try to juxtapose some sort of life or sincerity onto a tougher musical edge that normally wouldn't fit together. You wouldn't hear Ministry going through what I go through. It's not intended to be in the Skinny Puppy vein, snarling and griping that the world sucks. It's not about politics or grandiose statements. It's more introspective. Internal decay and collapse happened to be my motivation at the time."

A key element that distinguished NIN from more orthodox industrial outfits was Reznor's accessible song structures. "I think something that sets NIN apart from other groups of its ilk is that as much as I try not to do it, I still end up writing in a pop-song vein. Also, I'm not coming from the same point of view as they are. I'm not saying it's better, it's just different. What I'm doing is taking a song and arranging it, rather than building up a groove and chanting over it."

Still, Nine Inch Nails's music was, by most industry standards, radical and decidedly uncommercial. Yet it almost immediately won approval from young music fans.

And, despite Reznor's reluctance to embrace the industrial tag, *Pretty Hate Machine* was quickly proclaimed by critics as a landmark in that loosely defined genre. The manically catchy "Head Like a Hole," released by TVT as the album's second single, exercised a level of influence that would lead many to cite it as an industrial-dance equivalent of "Smells Like Teen Spirit" (which hadn't actually been released yet). *Pretty Hate Machine* would eventually become the first "industrial" album to become a certified million-seller.

Despite the album's impressive commercial performance, Reznor continued to maintain that he saw Nine Inch Nails's commercial prospects as being distinctly limited. "I would have no problem with major success, so long as I feel I'm doing what I want to do," he told *Alternative Press*. "I want people to like it, but I'm not going to the extreme of putting out shitty, bland, radio-oriented music to get people to say, 'Oh, I like that.' If I can bend radio's ear to fit what I'm doing, great. If they won't bend, I'm not going to pump out shit. On the next album there may be a track they can play on modern rock radio. Maybe there won't be. I don't know, but it will be on my terms."

The "Down In It" single had been accompanied by a promotional video—produced by the Chicago-based team H-Gun, which had previously shot promo clips for Ministry and the Revolting Cocks. The clip proved to be an early omen of NIN's uncanny ability for attracting controversy. During the shoot, a camera tied to a helium balloon—in order to catch an overhead shot of Reznor playing dead—reportedly broke away from its moorings and floated away. As the story goes, the errant camera was eventually found by a farmer, who turned it in to the police who, viewing footage of the apparently lifeless Reznor, called in the FBI, who launched an investigation of the apparent "snuff" film.

After all that trouble, the finished video ran afoul of MTV's notoriously conservative screening process. The cable music network wouldn't accept the clip until all shots of the "dead" Trent were excised—much to Reznor's irritation. "Our video was edited because I'm lying dead at the end of it. I can see that on a soap opera in the middle of the day. It's nothing mortifying like I'm riddled with bullets or falling from a building. I'm just lying on the ground. (But) that implies suicide, and we can't have that on MTV. But we can have Cher's naked ass."

Among other things, this minicontroversy helped make it difficult for Reznor to explain his budding celebrity status to his beloved grandparents. "I try to tell them, 'You're not going to hear my music on the radio. I'm not going to be on soap operas singing this.' I can imagine what my grandfather tells people—'It's called Nine Inch Nails, here's the video. And here he is lying dead at the end of it.' I warned my grandfather that the church might be after him."

CHAPTER 5

Prior to Reznor's signing with TVT, Nine Inch Nails was almost exclusively a studio act, and a one-man studio act at that. So when faced with the dilemma of translating *Pretty Hate Machine* into the live-performance medium, Trent was understandably intimidated.

"I was from the Todd Rundgren school," he explained to *Spin*. "The studio is an instrument. Manipulate it, don't go in thinking it's got to sound like a band. When I got done with *Pretty Hate Machine*, I realized, 'Holy fuck, how am I going to play this live?' I knew I didn't want to go out and do a Nitzer Ebb, two guys standing there kicking pads. I like electronic music, and I hate that sort of thing. I also didn't want the record to be one nerd with a synthesizer, (or) for there to be a David Bowie-type backup band, fifteen people and a horn section. I use electronics because I want to—not as a compromise for something else.

"I didn't want to tour by myself because that would suck," he told *Alternative Press*. "And I didn't want to have it all be taped or sequenced. The idea of getting a band together that plays stuff live was interesting, but I thought, 'Will this music work with people playing it live versus a computer?' It was a choice to use computers in the first place. I like the sound that they make more than people in some cases. I was trying to strike the right balance between what was live and what was sequenced and still trying to maintain the electronic feel."

Reznor had originally planned to go to England to audition players for a live band. He had even considered relocating there to distance himself from the provincial Cleveland scene, which he viewed as petty and unsupportive. He placed musicians-wanted ads in some of England's weekly music papers, and received about a hundred responses. In the end, though, he decided that the most practical course of action would be to recruit young, impressionable musicians from the Cleveland scene and "mold them into whatever I wanted to use them for, instead of polished, great musicians who would come in with an attitude of 'It should be like this.' "

The local players chosen for the task of translating *Pretty Hate Machine* to live performance were longtime pal Chris Vrenna on drums, Richard Patrick on guitar and Nick Rushe (with whom Reznor had worked with in Exotic Birds) on keyboards; Rushe would soon be succeeded by David Haymes and then Lee Mars. Reznor's hands-on leadership was firmly established from the get-go.

"I'm not in the position to offer somebody a thousand dollars a week to rehearse," Reznor said. "So I took some young guys who were malleable, who would basically do what I want them to do but expand on it. The only context I've worked with them in so far is, 'Here are the songs, here are your parts, learn them.' When I start to do the next record, it'll be up in the air as to what happens. I don't see it becoming a democracy, ever.

"It's not a band," he continued. "It's not, 'Here's an idea for a song, let's all work on it.' I would hope someday that it would be more of a collaboration, but it isn't right now. It's basically, if you don't like what you're playing, come up with something better. If I like it, you can play it. If I don't, play what I did.

"Not to be a prick, but I have an idea of how I want things to come out, and it's tough when you're in a situation where you're not quite sure of someone's direction. I'm not thinking guitar part; I'm thinking of the part that fits the big picture. If it's guitar, fine; if it's cowbell, fine. If it sucks, then I've got myself to blame. Some people mistake it for egotism. I'm not out to say I played every part and I edited every piece of tape, but it just works out that way."

Rearranging the album's songs for the live band proved to be a major challenge, and one that would have a significant effect on Reznor's future studio recordings. "Since (*Pretty Hate Machine*) was all done on the computer, with a little bit of guitar, it was a struggle as to what kind of people should I use, what instrumentation should I use. I didn't want to go out with just a tapedeck and me, so I decided to arrange it with real drums, add another guitar player, I'll play guitar live, keyboard player. And to maintain the integrity of the electronic side of it . . . We worked out a way to play with tapes where a certain part of the music, like the bass for example and some loops and things that you don't need to see a person playing, or would be very difficult to play, like a sixteenth note pattern real fast for the whole song, put that on tape."

The mix of live instruments with prerecorded sounds and sequenced rhythms eventually revealed new depths in Reznor's compositions. "Much to my pleasure, after a few months of touring, it really started to work," Reznor told *Spin.* "The songs started to take on a new life."

The live band's growing confidence and forceful-ness—and the now dreadlocked, shaven-templed Reznor's maturation into a riveting frontman—was accelerated by the fact that NIN was breaking in its increasingly intense live act opening shows for headliners whose live presentation was something less than earthshaking. The Nails opened for English distorto-popsters The Jesus and Mary Chain between January and March of 1990, before supporting ex-Bauhaus frontman and goth godhead Peter Murphy beginning in April.

"Two headliners that weren't difficult to blow off the stage," Reznor assessed. "And then it took over. This weird fucking energy and negative-energy release, this purging exorcism that takes place onstage."

Nine Inch Nails shows were progressing rapidly into terrifying, confrontational spectacles, with the five-foot-seven Reznor—covered in cornstarch, clad in leather and wearing black lipstick and eyeliner—physically attacking his bandmates and smashing instruments in a choreographed frenzy whose cathartic release offset the rigidity of the songs' machine beats.

Like *Pretty Hate Machine*'s studio sound, the evolution of the antagonistic NIN stage show was the result of much trial and error. "We've experimented with playing standing still and concentrating on how well we play our instruments," Reznor said at the time. "Then we'll do a show where we can hardly stand up because we're so drunk and we're fucking up every song forgetting lyrics and I fall down or accidentally knock over the drums, the guitars and the keyboards, and we're the fucking best band they've ever seen.

"Our show got much more anger-oriented, or just fucking frustration-oriented, rather than 'We really want to do a fine job for everybody out there.' 'Fuck you, like our music or we're going to fucking spit beer on you and insult you.' When you do, they love you more and then that makes you have less respect for them. It just fuels itself to where you just turn into something else. It's a weird thing.

"You really have to get into combat mode to do this. After the first eighty shows there was the immediate feedback from the audience and just the grueling rigors of touring—not to sound like Bon Jovi or anything. It's fairly intense to get out there every night with this mindset to go out and attack. I just thought about this the other day—I've been drunk every night since January. I can't fake being mean. After a while it got more fun to be abusive to the crowd and then people began to like us more."

The Jesus and Mary Chain dates went smoothly, but the Murphy tour grew increasingly tense. As Trent explained to *Alternative Press*, "We were playing theaters and college auditoriums and places where you can't drink and there are these steroid freaks that will beat you for just speaking. That was the worst possible environment for us to be in.

"So the stage for us is really small because they have all these drum risers and lights. Now they had this light two feet behind where I stand. If you don't move it, there's a good chance I'm going to run into it. (Murphy's) crew was like 'Must you run into that with your antics?' We were doing two nights in Atlanta—which I hate anyway—and we get on stage and there's all this junk sitting there including a half-eaten pizza that we had at soundcheck. I got really drunk and I took this pizza and started firing it out into the audience. I had this great feeling hitting all these death-rocker guys in the head with all this cold pizza! We also had these boxes of cornstarch that we were covering ourselves in and we threw those into the audience as well. Then I smashed a guitar, knocked the drums over and walked offstage. And that's what it took to get that audience to like us. Forget the music, as soon as they got abused, that was it. We outsold Peter Murphy on T-shirts.

"As soon as I walked downstairs, I was attacked by keyboard roadies, guitar roadies, the tour managers screaming, 'What are you doing? We are going to throw you off this tour!' And I said, 'What's the problem? Kick us off, I could use a few weeks off.' So that ended with us not being friends anymore and nobody spoke to us for the last two weeks of the tour."

By the summer of 1990, Nine Inch Nails had a devoted enough following—and an exciting enough stage act—to justify a headlining tour of large clubs. For their opening act, they tapped influential English industrial combo Meat Beat Manifesto, a longtime Reznor fave.

"It was like, a nice upward curve of success," Reznor said of the roadwork the band did in support of *Pretty Hate Machine*. "And the neat thing that happened with the music was, it was live enough that it could mutate into whatever it would mutate into."

Meanwhile, Reznor continued to develop his increasingly commanding stage persona. "That's the me that's allowed to act," he told *Spin*. "There's this weird kind of energy that just pops up when we do a show. There's a level of connection that starts to happen.

"Maybe in an odd way," he reasoned, "there is a real human communication that ends up being positive even though everything being said is negative."

Years later, Reznor would look back on his first serious brush with touring as an eye-opening experience. "I remember when we were just starting out, we were opening for a couple of other bands and nobody knew who the fuck we were and MTV didn't give a shit about us and radio didn't really give a shit about us. I remember the first time I looked down and I could see people singing words back at me and it really seemed like they meant it. They're fucking yelling back at me and I'm yelling back at them and suddenly it seemed like it's starting to be worth it now. The fact that someone can relate to something you, in an intimate moment, jotted down, just blew me away."

Touring, he says, was also a revelation in other, non-musical ways. "It was the first time we'd ever acknowledged to another male that you actually masturbate," he told *Details*. "We all felt liberated, and then it finally got to

NINE INCH NAILS

the point where . . . we'd always room with two guys in a room, and there'd be the Masturbation Moment. You'd get the bathroom, and the deal was you wouldn't fuck with that person. It was, 'Look, I'm jacking off. It could be fifteen minutes, could be an hour. Take messages.' "

CHAPTER 6

Trent Reznor's musical aesthetic had been shaped to a great degree by the output of the Chicago-based Wax Trax! label, which had helped pioneer the style that would become known as industrial, and was the home of Ministry and the various side projects of the group's mastermind, Al Jourgensen. "If anyone ever asks me about influences I always say Ministry," said Trent.

In between the band's post-*Pretty Hate Machine* road trips, Reznor got the chance to work with his idol Jourgensen, who produced a Nine Inch Nails cover of an old Queen song, "Get Down, Make Love," which the band had been performing live; the track appeared as a B-side on NIN's third TVT single, "Sin."

New pals Reznor and Jourgensen also collaborated on a track for Jourgensen's side project 1000 Homo DJs, a cover of Black Sabbath's "Supernaut," with Trent on lead vocals. TVT was not pleased. "I foolishly told (TVT) and they created all kinds of problems for Wax Trax!, to the point where I finally told Al to redo it without me," Trent claimed. Actually, Jourgensen merely electronically altered Reznor's vocal to the point of unrecognizability. The original version, with Trent's undoctored vocal, later showed up as a bootleg single, and was eventually released legitimately on the Wax Trax! retrospective *Black Box* (by that time, record company conflicts had become irrelevant, since TVT had purchased Wax Trax!). Reznor's friendship with Jourgensen also led to the two working together with another popular industrial combo, the Revolting Cocks.

Trent also guested on *Gub*, the Steve Albini-produced album by Pigface, a side project/supergroup organized by Public Image Ltd./Killing Joke/Ministry drummer Martin Atkins (who'd also played a few live shows with NIN) and Ministry drummer Bill Rieflin. Trent sang and cowrote a new song, "Suck," as well as cowriting and contributing some production work to "The Bushmaster." Trent and Chris Vrenna also toured briefly as members of Pigface.

The opportunity to work with someone he admired as much as Jourgensen was a thrill for Trent, and the pair's studio collaborations coincided with Reznor's desire to dispel Nine Inch Nails's previous synth-band image and establish a more aggressive approach, much as Ministry had in the early eighties.

"The studio for Al is a multilevel experience," Reznor said admiringly. "It's not just recording. Some people work in the studio with just the artist, producer, an engineer. With Al, there could be thirty people there. . . . The last time I was up there was the night before we shot the ("Down In It") video. It was two A.M. and I just wanted to stop by for five minutes. I got home at about eight in the morning. 'Time to get up and shoot your new video!' Aaah, thanks, Al."

At the time, there was much speculation that Jourgensen might be involved in some capacity with the next Nine Inch Nails project, although Trent made it clear that Flood remained his producer of choice. "The general theory for the new record," he said in the March 1990 issue of *Alternative Press*, "is to make better songs with better hooks, but arranged in a less conventional manner, and to run some styles together you wouldn't normally think would work that well. This will probably once again keep us off all commercial radio. But that's what I want to do.

"The whole idea of NIN and the way it's going to evolve is it will be what I feel like and that's the justification for whatever it is. It has to be what I want to do and not 'You have to make this fucking Top 40.' That will never be the case—and if it is, don't buy the record. Teach me a lesson."

Despite the now firmly established power of his live band, Reznor made it clear that he still planned to handle all the playing himself. "It's just going to be me and Flood, more like a collaboration between producer and me. Not necessarily like a traditional band, just whatever I stumble across on the computer. Hopefully better songs. We'll see how it comes out. It should be quite different than this one, sonically. Outlook-wise, I don't know. We'll see how bummed out I am when I write.

"I've become a workaholic just because I have nothing else to do, really," he admitted to RIP. "As long as I keep working, I don't have to deal with every other aspect of my life."

But it would be awhile before he'd get to work on a new Nine Inch Nails record. Reznor's conflicts with TVT—and his personal disdain for Steve Gottlieb—had grown beyond resolvability. Reznor's much-publicized efforts to escape his contract with the label would keep him out of recording action until the dispute was sorted out.

CHAPTER 7

With Nine Inch Nails's next studio project on indefinite hold due to his disputes with TVT, Trent Reznor had little choice but to continue playing live. "We had to keep touring to pay our legal costs," he claimed.

In some respects, that frustrating circumstance would turn out to be a blessing in disguise. The band spent much of the summer of 1991 as a low-billed act on the first Lollapalooza tour, on which they consistently stole the thunder of headliners Jane's Addiction, as well as consistently outselling them at the merchandise booths.

The Lollapalooza crowds' rapturous reception to Reznor and company's seemingly anarchic yet carefully staged orgies of tortured vocals, pummeling machine beats and squalling feedback—all delivered at brain-jarring volume levels—added up to a unique multisensoral assault.

As *Rolling Stone* described the scene at the time, "Monstruous electronic disco beats washed with jungle drums and shrieking feedback guitar were so loudly amplified that it actually felt a couple of degrees cooler when the music stopped for a bit between songs. Even Reznor's backup musicians looked terrified. It was as close to the anarchic assault of primo rock 'n' roll as it is possible for, er, disco to get."

The Lollapalooza shows saw Jeff Ward, a veteran of such noted industrial outfits as Ministry, the Revolting Cocks and Lard, replacing Vrenna (who'd had a temporary falling out with Reznor and briefly joined Stabbing Westward). Another new addition to the lineup was keyboardist James Woolley, who'd previously worked with the Chicago industrial combo Die Warzau.

Although NIN's increasingly intensive live sets had already won over crowds on the Jesus and Mary Chain and Peter Murphy tours, it was Lollapalooza that truly established Nine Inch Nails as a force to be reckoned with.

Typically, Reznor expressed ambivalence about NIN's Lollapalooza success. "It was really weird going from being a fanzine-level band to outselling Jane's Addiction in merchandise sales at Lollapalooza. The bigger the stakes, the more uncomfortable and out of control it starts to feel.

"With Lollapalooza, we were still an up-and-coming thing," he later stated to *Musician.* "We're in front of this scary, potentially hostile audience of 25,000. I was afraid the other bands might be into this star thing. But everybody, with the exception of Henry Rollins, was totally friendly. I remember Ice-T playing guitar with us on 'Head Like a Hole,' totally cool guy, very talented.

"But it was a soul destroyer in terms of the technical problems we were having. My performance started revolving around dealing with what was fucking up rather than communicating with the audience. Plus this is the tail end of about two and a half years of touring, compounded by the fact that my drummer had a heroin problem. And other band members had traumas and I felt beaten up to the point where I was hiding, I couldn't deal with it. The lyrics from *Broken* started to form around then."

Additionally, the gulf between *Pretty Hate Machine*'s relative restraint and the live show's all-out assault had become uncomfortable for Reznor, particularly since the opportunity to make a new Nine Inch Nails record—one that would be more representative of the band's current direction—seemed increasingly remote.

Whatever Reznor's reservations, in concrete career terms, Lollapalooza was a triumph. "The entertainment factor of our show got proven at Lollapalooza. We'd filtered into mall culture a little bit."

Still, there were a few more dues yet to be paid, including a tour of Europe which included a disastrous stadium show in Germany as opening act for trouble-prone hard-rock bad boys Guns N' Roses, then at the height of their popularity.

"Axl Rose made contact with us," Trent recalled. "He was a fan, and wanted to help out. We were going to Europe to do a tour, and we figured out what better way to confuse people than to open for Guns N' Roses? So we did, and the audience hated us. We were terrified to start with, and then we're talking onstage in front of 65,000 people in Germany. The first song goes okay. Second song people realize we're not Skid Row, who came on after us. Third song they'd confirmed the fact that they've heard a synthesizer and it's time to *attack*.

"There's something about the sight of every single person flipping you off in a giant stadium that makes you go instantly numb. I started laughing, then insulted them with anything I could think of. At that moment I see this fucking link sausage come flying up onstage and I thought, 'Okay, Germany, link sausage, you got us.' So that was a penis shrinker. Then I looked into the audience and about twenty rows back there's some poor fucking kid holding up a NIN shirt, and I gave him a quick thumbs-up. Suddenly there was this scuffle and he was *gone*. Never to be seen again. That night we got the figures for our T-shirt sales. Out of 65,000 people, how many did we sell? Three.

"Then some idiot booked us on the stupidest tour of all time, opening for The Wonder Stuff," he continued. "I started drinking, which we never do when we play. . . . Then I knew I had to get out but I couldn't. The only way out was through the crowd back to the dressing room, and I struggled but people kept putting me back on stage. I looked down and our road manager's mouth was a bloody mess. I asked what happened, and he said, "You punched me four times in the mouth!' I freaked, had to get away from that scene and everything onstage was broken. It was just too much shit to deal with."

CHAPTER 8

"It's cool to be the underdog," Trent told U. magazine in 1994, "but when you start rising to the top, there's more people ready to drag you down any way they can."

Reznor has always maintained that TVT hated *Pretty Hate Machine* and gave little attention to Nine Inch Nails until the album's sales took off, and that Steve Gottlieb had tried to push the band in a more conventionally commercial direction than Reznor intended. He further asserted that the label had consistently misrepresented Reznor's artistic intentions through inappropriate or carelessly handled cover art and advertising. In addition, he cited various disputes over videos, singles and tour support, and claimed that he was owed royalties by the label.

It was during the Lollapalooza tour that the NIN/TVT feud escalated into a full-blown war, with Reznor refusing to communicate with the label while making hostile anti-TVT pronouncements in interviews.

In addition to disputing Reznor's accusations, Gottlieb suggests that his falling out with the artist may be the result of the actions of other individuals involved with Trent's career as well as Trent's natural antipathy toward authority.

"Trent was insulated by a manager and a lawyer who allowed him to have very little direct contact (with TVT)," Gottlieb claims, adding, "That went back to the very beginning. Trent's manager would never allow us to be alone with Trent. Not that it never happened, but there were very few instances when we were allowed to meet with Trent, and that increased as the project went along. It got **73** progressively harder to gain any kind of access. Anything at all that transpired was through intermediaries. . . .

"The whole thing got out of control. Obviously it's really personal for Trent, and it just took on a kind of life of its own. I think Trent got the impression that we were unappreciative of him and that, for whatever reason, any kind of dialogue or discussion was taken as a threat to his autonomy.

"Trent's only correspondence to me, prior to *Pretty Hate Machine* being recorded, to kind of explain the record, was a ten-page letter explaining the lyrics and the songs and what he's about as an artist and his dreams and ambitions. He signed it 'Your Paycheck.' "

Gottlieb doesn't see greed on Reznor's part as the reason behind Reznor's attempt to escape his TVT contract. "Trent's not about greed. . . . I think Trent fully believes, and very passionately, that I've done things wrong. But he's never expressly said *what* it is. To the extent that he has suggested things in the press, they have been untrue."

Though Gottlieb does acknowledge a dispute over the purchase of some recording equipment—which he attributes to a simple misunderstanding—he denies Reznor's claims that the label witheld tour support and royalties. "I think he's been misled over that," Gottlieb says. "There were no disputes over royalties. He did an audit and the audit found that he had been overpaid. They had a handful of issues in terms of accounting, and when you're dealing with a lot of numbers, differences come up. His big claim under the audit was that 'Head Like A Hole,' which was labeled as an EP and sold as an EP, his auditor said it should have been treated like an album and he should have gotten an album royalty, even though he knew from the beginning that it was never signed, labeled or sold as an album."

Though he admits that he did attempt to convince Reznor to feature the NIN logo more prominently in *Pretty Hate Machine*'s cover art, Gottlieb strongly disputes the claim that TVT misrepresented his artistic vision via inappropriate cover art and advertising. "He had control," Gottlieb insists. "His artist created the album cover and the single covers; all the album art and packaging was created by Trent's own person.

"We took a lot of steps because we knew Trent was going to be a superstar," Gottlieb states. "We knew that everything needed to be documented, because at some point in time Trent would come back and want to know where all the money was spent. For example we wanted to make sure his manager kept good records of how tour support was spent, (so) we asked him to file reports on it. The management really objected to that, and this was taken as kind of an affront to Trent, when it was really trying to do something to protect him."

Still, it was obvious that the dispute took a heavy toll on Reznor. "I basically had a nervous breakdown," he told *Request*. "I realized that as cool as Nine Inch Nails was, it was probably over at that point because we were in a real bad situation with the label, which I'll just say completely repressed me in every way artistically. There was no way I could do another album. The average person may not realize how concerned I am with how Nine Inch Nails appears, in terms of what our covers look like. When you're hooked up with a company that is doing everything they can to push you in a direction you don't feel comfortable with, everything becomes a big issue."

It was obvious that Reznor was beginning to buckle under the unforeseen pressures that came along with success. "If you'd asked me before *Pretty Hate Machine* what my ideal career would be, I'd have said that three or four records in, I'd like a gold record," he later observed. "I'd have time to hone my craft and get an audience that, over time, would grow. If I had to pick a career I'd like to mimic, it'd be the Cure, or Depeche Mode even. They've pretty much stuck to their guns and their audiences have grown steadily. I thought (*Pretty Hate Machine*) was really good for the time, and I still do. But when it came out, I had very modest expectations. Plus, TVT thought it sucked and told me if I sold 20,000 it would be a miracle."

Gottlieb flatly denies the latter allegation. "I think it should be clear from everything we did that we loved it and fought for it."

He further points out that TVT spent considerable time, energy and money working to promote the album and establish Reznor as an artist of significance. "Breaking Nine Inch Nails was not an easy matter," says Gottlieb. "We started the largest campaign that an independent label had ever put toward an artist. I would personally go to MTV and to magazine editors and say 'If you're not playing this artist, you're just not aware of what's happening in music today.' I put my name and the name of the company on the line. After the first six or eight months of marketing, we had sold some 20,000 units and gone Top Ten on the alternative chart and Top Ten on the college chart, and we had a Top Ten dance single.

"At that (time), for a debut by what was considered to be an industrial artist, that was considered success. Many labels would have said 'That's fine, on to the next album.' But we put our heads down and continued to work this record for the next two-and-a-half, three years. By the time Trent played Lollapalooza, his record had already surpassed Ministry and was the biggest-selling record in the (industrial) genre. It had already sold 350,000 copies, which—prior to Nirvana breaking alternative music to the masses—was a very big accomplishment."

"I drove (TVT staff) people crazy because I made them call the same people over and over again, and told them to keep working it. We spent money that we had no hope of getting back, to build (Trent's) image. We really devoted ourselves to building a scene. We not only did regular videos, we did extended videos, and did a tremendous amount of grass-roots marketing. They were part of building an artist (on a longterm basis), as opposed to just making it back on the next record. . . . We took national TV spots all over the place to help consolidate the growing support for Trent. We did a hundred different innovative marketing things.

"We acquitted our role, in my mind, extremely well," Gottlieb concludes. "Had Trent been signed to a major record company, they would have never hung in and spent the time it took to break him through, they would have said 'That's fine' and left well enough alone. And if it had been another indie, they probably would have never underwritten the project and given unlimited tour support and unlimited videos and all the rest of it."

His experiences with TVT heightened Reznor's pessimism about the music industry. "It's made me see a really horrendous side of the music business. (I) realized that it's just a big slavery system, and I'm just a cog in this wheel of machinery. And it's not about art, it's about who can sell the most units, and how can we manipulate this audience to like this, and I've realized that the next Nine Inch Nails record may never come out."

Weary from his ongoing battles with his label, Trent had begun publicly making noises about quitting recording altogether, swearing that he'd sooner retire than ever make another record for Steve Gottlieb. Reznor's statements regarding his disillusionment and frustration during this period certainly carry the ring of truth.

"I've got (the next record) half written, I know what it's about, it's ready to go," he said at the time. "But we've had so much trouble with (TVT), that a giant lawsuit is about to begin. And I just made the decision myself. The only reason I got into this in the first place was to have some sort of integrity. . . . Now I'm at the point where I'm being raped, and I can't do this because . . . and I can't say this word (in a song) because you can't get it played on the radio, and we're going to decide who does your next video and shit like that, and I can't do that. I can't put up with that."

Gottlieb denies that TVT interfered with Reznor creatively. "We were exceptionally excited by him as an artist, and gave him the wherewithal to make the most expensive debut record by anyone in the genre at that time. He was given complete creative freedom, and worked with all the producers that he wanted to work with in all the studios that he wanted to work in."

Gottlieb adds, however, that he's proud of TVT's contribution to *Pretty Hate Machine*. "Some people have reported it as if Trent delivered a finished album, and that our involvement was only to press it up and ship it out. Our involvement, and the support we gave to his vision, was far greater and much more involved in that. I personally took him over to the U.K. to help get him set up there; he'd never traveled abroad before. I was involved in going up to Boston and introducing him to Flood. To the extent that (TVT) were involved creatively in that record, we were proud of everything that we did to help shape it."

In any event, it was obvious that Reznor was fed up. As he later told *Musician*, "When I got off the road after the *Pretty Hate Machine* and Lollapalooza tours, I didn't write a note of music and I wasn't sure I wanted to do it anymore, to be honest with you."

With Reznor's relationship with TVT seemingly

beyond repair and possibility of expensive and time-consuming litigation pending, Nine Inch Nails's life as a recording act was at an impasse—contractually unable to record for anyone else and refusing to make another album for TVT.

Fortunately, *Pretty Hate Machine*'s platinum sales and the group's scene-stealing Lollapalooza performances had established Nine Inch Nails as a hot industry property. But, even if Nine Inch Nails was to make the move to another label, the decision of where and how didn't necessarily rest in Reznor's hands. The situation was resolved when Interscope Records—a young, WEA-distributed label which at the time had had its major successes with considerably less edgy acts like Marky Mark and Gerardo—entered the picture.

"We kind of got slave-traded," Reznor remarked to *Spin*. "It wasn't my doing, I didn't know anything about Interscope. And I was real pissed off at first because it was going from one bad situation to potentially another one. But Interscope went into it like they really wanted to know what I wanted. It was good—after I put my raving lunatic act on."

According to Gottlieb, "Faced with a relationship that was imperfect, we had several choices. We could have just had a lawsuit, which we felt we would win. Or we could have auctioned off our contract rights to the highest bidder and gotten the most amount of cash. The trade-off of being right and having justice vs. seeing the artist's career fulfilled wasn't a good one. But selling off the artist in some kind of bidding war wasn't right either, because we knew this was an artist who needs a lot of attention.

"We thought that Trent would be doing backflips (over the Interscope deal). We did a deal where we agreed that we would step totally aside, and if Trent never wanted to talk to me again, he wouldn't have to talk to me again. Here he was gonna be able to get himself a superstar deal on his second album, we weren't gonna hold him to his contract. All of a sudden he was gonna be treated like a superstar, put millions of dollars in his pocket, get a superstar royalty. It was something that we thought he would love, and ultimately he *does* love it.

"But it took awhile," Gottlieb adds. "Trent wouldn't talk to Interscope for six months, and it took him a full year to get comfortable with what the joint venture was offering."

Gottlieb staunchly defends his company's role in Nine Inch Nails's early career. "We've acted in good faith and I think have done a great job for Trent, not only in terms of what we did in helping him make *Pretty Hate Machine* and the various singles, not only in terms of presenting them to the marketplace in a way that was consistent with his wishes as an artist, and in coming up with the joint venture as a good solution to resolving it, that allows him to get on with his life as an artist. And it's also made him a ton of money."

Under the new arrangement, Interscope would deal with the hands-on aspects of A&R marketing, promotion and distribution, and TVT would receive a percentage of

Nine Inch Nails' future record sales, approve various expenditures and out-of-joint profits with Interscope funding some of Trent's projects, like Nothing Records.

Trent told *Axcess* that he could live with TVT keeping a portion of his earnings "as long as it's hidden from me and I don't have to deal with them. It disgusts me. It makes me sick to think that they still get money from me, but as long as I don't have to see them or deal with them . . . "

Unbeknownst to TVT or Interscope, Reznor and Flood had been recording in virtual secrecy at Miami's South Beach Studios, and the new material would become Nine Inch Nails's first Interscope release, *Broken*. "Flood and I had to record *Broken* under a different band name," Trent claimed in an interview with *Spin*, "because if TVT found out we were recording, they could confiscate all of our shit and release it."

Though the rest of Nine Inch Nails's live lineup wasn't involved in the recording, *Broken* made good on Reznor's intention of finally bringing NIN's recording approach into synch with the uncompromising spirit of the band's live shows. Indeed, the disc moved Nine Inch Nails into new vistas of aural brutality, offering a harrowingly dissonant, largely guitar-based wall of sound that provided a perfect vehicle for the unfocused but nonetheless potent stew of hate, misery and despair that comprised the lyrics of Trent's new compositions. The lyrics of songs like "Wish," "Gave Up" and the record's centerpiece "Happiness In Slavery" were inspired partially by an ill-fated romance and largely by Reznor's bitter hatred of

Steve Gottlieb, whom he perceived as having nearly destroyed his career.

"On a personal level, I was coming out of a weird relationship," he told *Spin*. "I really fell in love with someone and we lived together for six or eight months. But it went from being the best to the worst. Plus, I hadn't spoken to (TVT) since before Lollapalooza. We made it very clear we were not doing another record for TVT. But they made it pretty clear that they weren't ready to sell. So I felt like, well, I've finally gotten this thing going but it's dead.

"My whole life became my career, essentially. And then I was faced with the fact that my career could easily have been over because the people that controlled it are fucking assholes. It's a horrible feeling. On one hand, Nine Inch Nails had a platinum album. And on the other hand I thought it was over because I was not doing another album for Gottlieb. And I was told litigation would have taken two years. That's where a lot of the rage on *Broken* comes from."

But the hatred that motivated *Broken*'s songs wasn't reserved strictly for the outside world: "*Pretty Hate Machine* was written from the point of view of someone who felt that the world may suck, but I like myself as a person and I can fight my way out of this bullshit. *Broken* introduced self-loathing, which is not a popular topic with anybody, especially in a song."

Broken's more extreme sonic approach was an accurate reflection of Nine Inch Nails's progression as a live act, which by the time of Lollapalooza had far outdistanced the comparative restraint of *Pretty Hate Machine*'s relatively conventional dance beats. "When we played the songs live they mutated, they got heavier and more rock oriented because of the live drums and guitars, and the sound began to take on a life of its own. A lot of people had seen us live and said we were great—then they went, 'God, I bought your record and it sucks, man! It's like some synth shit or something.' After hearing that so many times you start getting macho about it—'I'm gonna make the hardest-sounding record I can.' "

Broken certainly lived up to Reznor's goal of using state-of-the-art technology to make his music as raw and abrasive as possible, both sonically and lyrically. "The starting point was to make a dense record," Reznor told *Musician*, adding that his intention was to make "the kind of record that sounds like a real band playing, but upon further investigation there's something definitely wrong with it."

Reznor further explained that he and Flood intentionally layered more sonic information than the human ear could immediately process. "If we had forty-eight tracks, we wanted to bury forty-eight riffs that were meant to come out with repeated listenings."

"I wanted to be tough," Reznor later told *Spin*. "I was so concerned about staying 'alternative,' that indie bullshit mentality. After Lollapalooza, I had this snotty elitist mentality—you're not cool enough to like my band, don't buy my records. I wanted to make a 'fuck you' record. It was also a bit of a knee-jerk 'I'm not a pussy, I'm not a sell-out' attitude."

In addition to its six main tracks, Broken incorporated two additional numbers, a NINified cover of an old Adam Ant song, "Physical," and a newly recorded, somewhat blues-rockier version of "Suck," Trent's earlier contribution to the Pigface album; these two were originally intended to comprise a twelve-inch single that was supposed to be released by TVT to coincide with Lollapalooza, but went unreleased due to Reznor's disputes with the label.

Depending on what configuration of Broken one owned, the two bonus tracks could be heard in various ways. The first 250,000 U.S. copies of Broken were packaged with an additional three-inch CD containing the two tracks, while subsequent pressings would include the two songs as "hidden" bonus tracks, numbered 98 and 99 and appearing after a five-minute gap following the six main numbers. Meanwhile, some twelve-inch vinyl editions included the extra songs on a separate seven-inch single, while others put the six main songs on one side and the bonus pair on the flip.

Incidentally, "Physical" included at least one gratuitous swipe by Reznor at his former employer; at one point, Trent can be heard whispering "Eat your heart out, Steve."

Despite its ostensible inaccessibility, Broken was an instant hit upon its release in the fall of 1992. It quickly hit the national Top 10, and garnered largely positive reviews (Los Angeles Times critic Robert Hilburn, the epitome of mainstream critical respectability, even referred to Reznor as "rock's most compelling new antihero"), and eventually won a Grammy for the track "Wish"—ironically enough, in the category of Best Metal Performance.

Reznor is quick to dismiss the latter honor. "The best thing about it," he quips, "was that it's the only song to ever win a Grammy that says fist fuck in the lyrics."

Indeed, Reznor was keenly aware of the irony inherent in a record as brazenly anticommercial as *Broken* achieving mainstream success. "When I put (*Broken*) out, I thought I'd alienate every one of my fans, and I think subconsciously I wanted to because I'd just had enough," he mused in *Request*. "For that, I got a Grammy."

Broken's commercial success justified Interscope's faith in Reznor. Apparently, the feeling was mutual, as Trent expressed none of the animosity that he'd felt for his previous label. "As fate would have it, Interscope has been really cool," he said. "They give me money to do a record and let me do it. We work outside of them and basically treat them as a distributor. They show respect for me and my work, which I appreciate."

CHAPTER 9

No singles were released from *Broken,* since it was technically an EP rather than an album. But the collection did spawn several videos, which for the most part remain unseen—at least through legitimate channels—by fans, thanks to Reznor's insistence on exploring the visual equivalent of NIN's musical extremes.

The most notorious of these was a clip for "Happiness In Slavery," which has been widely cited as the most shockingly graphic thing in the history of music video. The genuinely disturbing piece, shot in black and white by director Jonathan Reiss, depicts performance artist Bob Flanagan (who has since died of cystic fibrosis), being voluntarily strapped, naked and blindfolded, into a mechanical contraption that systematically sexually assaults, mutilates and kills him. To no one's surprise, it was categorically rejected by MTV and virtually every other broadcast outlet.

Though he now classifies the "Happiness In Slavery" video as "not great," Reznor admits to taking pleasure in the furor surrounding its release. "It wasn't a conscious decision to make the most vulgar thing we could do to get press, which it could easily be attacked as being. But it was a chance for me to finally be able to do something I wanted without having to ask someone who has no fucking idea. The question came up: How far can we take this? I said, 'Let's just take it as far as we think is right. Forget that it's a music video, forget standards and censorship.' Fortunately or unfortunately, depending on how you look at it, it's unplayable. **89**

"We knew when we were doing it that we were going to go too far, that we would be beyond the limits of what was playable (on) American television, but it was interesting to us. When it was done, we considered, for maybe ten minutes, editing it to be seen. . . . But it just seemed like the right thing to do, and it was the thing I wanted to do. It expressed the song the best way it could. It wasn't a calculated idea to get somebody's penis in a video.

"The incentive behind it was not, 'Let's make a video that's really gross so it'll shock people.' It was that I finally had the freedom to do what I wanted to do. If it pisses somebody off or someone's offended by it, then at least there's some degree of response."

Though it wasn't widely shown through legitimate channels, bootleg dubs of the "Happiness In Slavery" video have been widely circulated amongst NIN fans. The controversial clip's underground notoriety has been strong enough to earn director Reiss something of a cult following that led to his being tapped for other extreme assignments, including an infamous (and rarely shown) clip for Danzig's "It's Coming Down."

Peter "Sleazy" Christopherson, a member of the influential English industrial/atmospheric trio Coil, directed somewhat less upsetting videos for "Wish" and "Pinion." The former depicts the band inside an elaborately constructed cage, surrounded by a ravenous crowd that eventually breaks through and attacks the group. The latter follows water from a flushed toilet through pipes and eventually into the mouth of a bound torture victim.

Despite "Pinion's" relatively mild content, MTV rejected it too (although it was shown, unedited, on the network's late-night alt-rock showcase *120 Minutes*). According to Trent, "MTV's reason for rejecting it was 'We can't show the human form in any sort of bondage.' My response: 'What about Madonna?' (Their) response: 'Madonna is Madonna.' "

Even more notorious than the "Happiness In Slavery" video is the unreleased long-form video compilation *Broken Movie*. The collection, directed by Christopherson, combined previously shot individual videos with a harrowing wraparound narrative involving a hostage who is forced to watch Nine Inch Nails videos, tortured and eventually killed in a manner that was so starkly realistic that *Broken Movie* was widely (and inaccurately) branded as a "snuff" film. Naturally, it was widely bootlegged and became another colorful chapter in NIN's rapidly evolving outlaw mythos.

Trent later described *Broken Movie* as "the most horrific thing you'll ever see," adding "I didn't put it out because I didn't want to spend the next five years explaining the thing to every reporter I meet. It makes 'Happiness In Slavery' look like a Disney movie."

Broken's release was followed a couple of months later by *Fixed*, a limited-edition companion disc featuring remixed, remodeled versions of the songs on *Broken*, by a variety of Reznor friends and associates. "I gave various people I respect full creative control to destroy any aspect of the original song and see what happens," explained Trent. "The record is not meant to be a grand statement of a new direction, it's just a twelve inch."

The remixes ranged from fascinating variations to barely recognizable wholesale overhauls. Jim "Foetus" Thirlwell added a driving, almost military drum track and a serene choral/orchestral bridge to "Wish," and oversaw a second "Wish" mix entitled "Fist Fuck," which extends the martial drum beats while scrambling the song's original structure into an abstract array of noises and spoken-word samples (incidentally, the snippet of dialogue in the song is from the movie musical *Showboat*).

Elsewhere on *Fixed*, Coil and Danny Hyde's recasting of "Gave Up" chopped Reznor's original vocal into something unearthly and indecipherable. "Happiness In Slavery" appeared in a synth-heavy, somewhat more linear reworking by Trent and Chris Vrenna that suggested what the song might sound like if it had been included on *Pretty Hate Machine*. "Happiness In Slavery" was also reworked into "Screaming Slave," an eight-minute electrical storm of noise and effects. And "Throw This Away" was a two-part epic—with different sections handled by Nirvana/Garbage producer Butch Vig and the Reznor/Vrenna team—that begins with brooding, atmospheric calm and builds to a relentless climax.

CHAPTER 10

Having spent a couple of years on the road supporting *Pretty Hate Machine*, Trent Reznor chose not to tour behind *Broken*. Instead, he dove directly into Nine Inch Nails's next recording effort, an ambitious full-length album about which he'd already formulated some very definite ideas.

After *Broken*'s cathartic but scattershot emotional purging, Reznor decided that his next step should be something more cohesive and emotionally well-rounded. What he had in mind was a concept album of sorts, to be titled *The Downward Spiral*. But whatever the conceptual forethought that went into the project, the album's creation would be a drawn-out, painful process fully in keeping with the atmosphere of emotional upheaval that was central to the album's creative focus.

"This album literally sucked the life out of me," Reznor would later say, and the fourteen-song collection's juxtaposition of gut-wrenchingly personal lyrics and frequently harrowing soundscapes bear witness to the psychic turmoil that Reznor went through to bring his vision to life.

"The idea for this record," he said in an interview with the Canadian music-video channel MuchMusic, "came about the end of '91 when we finished the first Lollapalooza, and we went to Europe. I was sitting in the hotel room and I was kind of seeing the energy that Nine Inch Nails was drawing upon. It was a definite negative vibe . . . So, this record was focusing on those certain things that were bothering me that I felt needed exploring." **95**

He'd also noticed that writing songs about his depressions had seemingly begun to feed rather than exorcise them. "I did reach a point where I thought I needed to get help," he told *USA Today*. "I couldn't turn my brain off. I talked to some friends who described exactly how I was feeling. They got on Prozac, but the idea of going on a drug that would shut my brain off doesn't appeal to me. My strategy of working things out of my system is not to ignore them, but to explore them, to shed light on them.

"After (*Broken*) came out, I wanted to start right away on a real album," Trent recalled in a *Spin* cover story. "I had been working on the idea of *Downward Spiral* in my head for a while without writing any songs, just a concept . . . I wrote down a bunch of topics I wanted to address. And key events in my life . . . Weird little displaced memories that conjure up emotions. Not always upsetting or unhappy. I remember walking home from piano lessons at age ten, twelve, a weird, euphoric feeling. Life is good. So in my notebook there was this huge page of stuff."

While Reznor wanted the album to explore new emotional territory, he was also determined that it should once again redefine the sonic and compositional parameters of Nine Inch Nails. "I didn't have a definite idea of how it should sound," he told *Keyboard* magazine. "I mean, I had a theme lyrically and vibe-wise, but musically I wanted to put more emphasis on textures and mood, and not rely on the same bag of tricks. I had to develop a whole new palette of sounds to work with."

"It was also a decision to get away from verse/chorus/verse/chorus/middle/verse/chorus/end," he explained to *Musician*. "Every song I'd ever written had that structure." He noted the influence of David Bowie's seminal 1977 album *Low* in inspiring him to diverge from traditional song structures. "Some of those songs you start listening to and it fades out and you say, 'That's weird. Were there any vocals in that?' "

By the spring of 1992, Reznor had left his adopted hometown of Cleveland—a city he perceived as being largely unsupportive of him and his music—for the more free-spirited environs of New Orleans. He had fallen in love with the Crescent City on a visit the year before, and planned to set up NIN's permanent base of operations there, complete with a studio where he had intended to record *The Downward Spiral*. But, after a proposed real estate deal in New Orleans fell through, he temporarily relocated to Los Angeles, planning to rent a house where he'd bring in recording equipment and set up a makeshift studio.

To that end, Reznor rented the infamous Bel Air house where actress Sharon Tate and four friends were murdered by members of Charles Manson's psychotic "family" in 1969. Given the artist's well-known taste for the macabre, the location would seem perfect for Nine Inch Nails activity. But Reznor insists that he was initially unaware of the house's grisly history.

"On a whim, I came out to Los Angeles," he recalled. "I looked at maybe fifteen houses in one day, and at that time I had no idea one of them was the Tate house. No one brought that to my attention, even though they should have.

"When I rented the place I didn't even realize it was

that house. When I found out I thought it was kind of interesting. I didn't think 'Oh, it'll be spooky to tell people that . . . ' I don't idolize Charles Manson, and I don't condone murdering people because you're a fucked-up hippie trying to make a statement. But it's an interesting little chapter in American history that it was cool to be a part of.

"The first night was *terrifying*," he admitted. "By then, I knew all about the place; I'd read all the books about the Manson murders. So I walked in the place at night and everything was dark, and I was like, 'Holy Jesus, that's where it happened.' Scary. I jumped a mile at every sound—even if it was an owl. I woke up in the middle of the night and there was a coyote looking in the window at me. I thought, 'I'm not gonna make it.'

"But after about a month I realized that if there's any vibe up there at all, it's one of sadness. It's not like spooky ghosts fucking with you or anything—although we did have a million electrical disturbances. Things that shouldn't have happened did happen. Eventually we'd just joke about it: 'Oh, Sharon must be here. The fucking tape machine just shut down.'

"Actually, it's a really beautiful place," Reznor said of the Tate house, which he somewhat tastelessly nick-named "Le Pig," in reference to the fact that the killers had smeared the word "*pig*" in the victims' blood on the house's walls. "The view from the front door is the best view of L.A. I've ever seen. It's amazing how beautiful looking down into a smog pit can be."

One of his reasons for recording in a home set-up rather than a conventional studio, he told *Keyboard*, was "I wanted to fine-tune my engineering skills . . . I figured if I had a studio around, I'd inevitably figure out how to do it. For the first time, we had the resources to do something right, so we ended up buying a big console and a couple of Studer machines because it was cheaper than renting, in the long run."

Despite his satisfaction with the new gear, a variety of delays conspired to keep *The Downward Spiral* from progressing at the pace Reznor had originally intended. "We moved out (to L.A.) on July 4, 1992," he explained. "What we thought would take X-amount of time to get a studio set up, ended up taking three times as long. As much as I enjoy equipment, fucking around with stuff, systems and all that, there came a point when the whole focus was just to get the damn thing working and then learn it.

"Another thing that delayed this record," he continued, "was me learning how to write again, deciding what I wanted to do. I didn't want to make another *Broken*. And I didn't want to go completely back to the *Pretty Hate Machine* style, percolating synth stuff."

Reznor had originally committed to deliver the album to Interscope in early 1993. But he quickly ran up against a severe case of writer's block, unable to produce anything he found satisfactory. "I was working for the wrong reasons, just to get it done and get out of L.A. and tour," he explained to *Request*.

Through the rest of 1993, Trent's new corporate patrons at Interscope expressed increasing concern about the project's tardiness, but Reznor refused to be swayed by the demands of expediency. "I get bored when people start saying, 'Where's the record already?' Hey, I'm not fucking off in there. It just takes a long time. Nirvana may be able to make a record in two weeks. That's great. We're not doing that. To me, every song means reinventing the whole process. There are no constants, except maybe that I'll sing it. But are the rhythm tracks going to be played or sequenced? Are they going to be real, fake, machines, drums, sounds, car doors slamming? It's not a simple matter of yelling out chords to someone across the room and starting the tape machine. It's a different situation. I'm not saying that makes my record any better than theirs. It's just a different set of parameters."

Some helpful input came from producer and Def American label chief Rick Rubin. Reznor later reported to *Rolling Stone*, "I'd been talking to Rick Rubin a lot—Rick's a pretty good friend of mine. And I was completely bummed out. Rick asked me what my motivation for doing this record was, and I told him the truth: Just to get it fucking done. And he said, 'That's the stupidest fucking reason for doing an album I've ever heard. Don't do it. Don't do it until you make music that it's a crime not to let other people hear.'

"I started thinking about it, and I realized he was right. I was in the most fortunate situation I could imagine. I had a decent budget for the record. I've got really cool equipment and a studio to work at. And for the first time, recording music was my job . . . I didn't have to fucking clean toilets all day just to afford a few minutes in the studio. So I kind of got my head back straight. I started noodling around with ideas, and five or six months later I've got two-thirds of a record written. It's like I came up for air."

CHAPTER 11

Given the magnitude of the creative challenge that Reznor had presented himself with, it's not surprising that *The Downward Spiral*'s birth cycle was something less than smooth. "I wanted it to be a departure from *Broken,* (which was) a real hard-sounding record that was just one big blast of anger," he explained to *Guitar World.* "This time I wanted to make an album that went in ten different directions, but was all united somehow. I didn't want to box Nine Inch Nails into a corner, where everything would be faster and harder than the last record, where every song had to say, 'Look how tough we are.' I don't think that's really me . . . Or rather, there are lots of times when I'll come up with musical ideas that don't fit that mold.

"On this record, I was more concerned with mood, texture, restraint and subtlety, rather than getting punched in the face four hundred times. Also I was trying to make a record that followed an evolving lyrical theme. I came up with a basic theme and said, 'Okay, let's divide that into ten or twelve slots.' But in trying to write songs to fill those slots, a lot of the ideas, of course, got modified. Many times, what was meant to be a down moment lyrically wound up going with music that was really the opposite of that.

"Probably the biggest influence on *The Downward Spiral* was David Bowie's *Low* album," he continued. "Actually, all his stuff from *Hunky Dory* through *Scary Monsters.* Plus old Lou Reed, Iggy Pop—stuff that I'd never really heard before, because I was listening to new wave at the time. But you compare a record like *Low* to any assortment of the Top 100 records at Tower right now, and the amount of craftsmanship and depth are much higher."

With Flood coproducing once again, the *Downward Spiral* studio team also included mixer Alan Moulder and Jane's Addiction/Porno for Pyros drummer Steve Perkins, who laid down some raw drum tracks that Reznor sampled to construct the album's percussion loops.

Also involved was Chris Vrenna who, back in the NIN fold, had taken on an active part in the recording process. "His role in the studio," Trent explained to *Request*, "is more an assistant than anything. If we need a drum set taken into thirty different rooms and sampled, he'll do that. He'll listen to five movies a day looking for ambience that evokes a texture. But most importantly, he understands where I'm coming from."

The most surprising participant in the *Downward Spiral* sessions was versatile guitar hero Adrian Belew, whose prodigious instrumental skills and self-effacing personality have endeared him to such stellar collaborators as David Bowie, Frank Zappa, Talking Heads and King Crimson. Reznor, who with uncharacteristic effusiveness refers to Belew as "an inspiration," recounts, "The songs were pretty much arranged, but we thought, 'What would it be like if we got someone in here who could really play his ass off?' "

Reznor and Flood brought Belew in for a marathon two-day tracking session, during which the guitarist was encouraged to let his improvisational creativity run wild. "It happened he was in L.A., and agreed to come up to the house the next day, so our bluff was called and we were intimidated. What are we going to do? We figured we'd just put on six songs and have him play through them. So Adrian shows up—totally nice guy, no attitude. But I could tell he was thinking, 'What am I doing here?' We were in the living room where Sharon Tate was murdered, the vibes started . . . what's going on here?"

The first song they had Belew play against was the shriekingly thrashy "Mr. Self Destruct." "We rolled the tapes and just asked him to play. He's, 'Do you want rhythm stuff?' I said, 'Anything you feel like doing.' 'Well, what key is it in?' 'Uh, I'm not sure, probably E, see what happens, don't worry about it.' He said something about just doing something with Paul Simon, and we said, 'Okay, this is the anti-Paul Simon.' This totally fast machine thing kicks in, he stops for a minute and just starts playing and immediately all of our mouths drop open. Just to see someone who can play that well and tasteful. We stopped the tape and he thought we were mad at him or something. And I said, 'No, it's worth paying you just to watch you play, man.'

"We basically told Adrian, 'Just play whatever you want and we'll piece it together however we see fit. Maybe stuff from one song will fit into another.' We did about six or seven songs with four or five passes each. One time we'd tell Adrian something like, 'Concentrate on a rhythmic part.' Another time, 'Think in terms of countermelody.' Or, 'Think in terms of no pitch at all, just noise.' He pulled out a bunch of great sounds that he never gets to use."

The admiration was mutual. Said Belew, "Trent has

an astounding command of technology, old and new; he's such an intriguing person to work with." Belew wasn't familiar with Nine Inch Nails prior to the session. "But that may have actually helped in some way."

That free-spirited approach to noisemaking dominated the sessions, and helped Reznor gain increased confidence in his own guitar work, which is technically primitive but undeniably expressive.

"I'm not as intimidated by it as I was at one time," Reznor told *Guitar World*. " 'Cause I always thought I wasn't very good. So if I wrote a guitar part, I would say to myself, 'Every guitar player in the world is going to hear this part and think, 'Here's a real easy, stupid part.'' ' But nowadays I just find the guitar much more expressive than the keyboard. Just because of the interface, obviously—strings and randomness. I find it interesting to sample sounds from a guitar track and then process them to the point where the performance has randomness and expression, and the sound becomes something completely new."

As he pointed out to *Musician*, "There's a transcription of 'Wish' in some guitar magazine, and the best part was where they said, 'This middle section is virtually untranscribable.' All right, success! Now, that main riff has got to be the simplest thing in the world for any real guitar player. But a lot of them ask me how the hell I got that sound. The answer is, Don't read the instruction book! Fiddle around. The studio itself became a real instrument for me. I didn't really know how it worked, but that's where the naiveté factor kicks in. You do something 'wrong' and think, 'Wow, that sounds cool, why not try this instead?'

"Just like my guitar revelation. Everyone mikes the speaker. Why not plug the amp right into the board? That sounds crazy to some people, it's not technically a 'good sound.' Who cares? What some players might initially think was a godawful sound was inspiring to me and it fit what the track needed. You have to get past the barriers that come with training. I have a hard time working with engineers, Flood excepted, because they'll try to undo everything I've made sound a certain way because 'drums or guitar don't sound that way.' Now with computers I can create guitar parts that I couldn't sit down and play.

"On this album and *Broken* I played stuff right into the board and then into the computer, and manipulated it with programs that don't work in real time. Once it's in there, you can do things to it that have no equivalency in the real world. Like analyze the frequency and flip it upside-down. It takes maybe ten minutes for the Macintosh to process that cut, and you wind up with sounds that are different from anything you could get otherwise. I like the idea that there are guitar players out there trying to figure them out. Hopefully, that'll cause some misery."

While Reznor has always insisted that the lyrics are the most important things on his records, *The Downward Spiral* received an equal amount of attention and acclaim for its inventive arrangements and ambitiously constructed instrumental tracks, which provide an imposing sonic framework that's every bit as provocative as his often disturbing lyrics.

Much of Reznor's effectiveness as a studio auteur lies in his ability to draw new sounds or combinations of sounds from machinery. And despite the state-of-the-art gear he employs on Nine Inch Nails's records, he's always seemed more interested in employing technology toward unconventional ends. "Being a programmer I find it more interesting to find how these machines can do things they weren't meant to do," he told *Plazm*. "Usually that is a lot more rewarding than plugging something in, reading the manual and doing just what you're told."

He takes an equally unorthodox approach to recording his vocals. "Vocal distortion has become incredibly clichéd, but there are varying degrees of blending it in and different effects that can come across. I want people to be able to hear what I'm saying, but I'm not interested in the Phil Collins vocal sound. Maybe it's because I'm insecure about my vocals, but it's my record, and I'm gonna make it sound shitty if I want to."

Still, *The Downward Spiral*'s effectiveness was more than a matter of technical achievement. Where Reznor had begun his recording career revelling in the inhuman clatter of mechanized rhythms, on *The Downward Spiral* he strove to extract warmer-sounding music from his machines. "I think I was setting out to make a record that you might not realize is mostly synthetic," he told *Musician*. "When you sit down behind a drum machine and a computer, there's a very obvious way to use it, and if you read the instructions, the music comes out a certain way. A lot of people reject that because they don't want a Janet Jackson- or Gary Numan-sounding record. It's dismissed as unfashionable. And I was at a point where I'm thinking, maybe there's a reason every rock band has guitars, drums, real people playing them.

"So I started this album on the computer or keyboards, then I fleshed them out by bringing in some guitar. Because of my classical training, I feel more competent on keyboards. As soon as I put my hands on the piano the chord is far richer than the E or A bar chord when I naively play guitar. I know where that added bit of harmonic depth is on keyboard, and that's one thing I wanted to expand on with this album.

"The organic thing is true on a number of levels. This album focuses on decay, and I chose to use a lot more organic sounds, from real instruments to swarms of bees. I hired a guy whose job was to do nothing but sample those sounds. So there were these new textures. But the guitar is a more expressive instrument in many ways, you can get nuances that are very hard to simulate on keyboards, and especially samplers.

"I think it is an interesting time right now," Reznor commented to *Plazm*. "My grandfather—the car was being invented. Now, I find myself bitching about hard disk access time, and I can do a whole album on computer. It will be interesting to see what happens, but I think we will only benefit from access to information. It's a good thing, though it will be misused."

As for the controversial practice of sampling, without which Nine Inch Nails would be a very different animal, he commented, "I think that sound is sound. If somebody sampled a bit of something in an album of mine, that's cool. I don't give a shit about that. I think it's interesting how rap groups piece together things into new sounds. I'm into that."

Still, he added, "I do think that it's totally out of control now. Asshole major label lawyers are getting in on it, and realizing they can make money by ripping people off. If M.C. Hammer looped 'Head Like a Hole' and did a rap over it, it'd piss me off, and I think I should be compensated because it's my song. I think at a certain point there should be some degree of compensation.

"I've used a lot of samples, but I don't tell anyone where I got them. It's not identifiable. I'm not just looping someone else's music. I'm more interested in textures than the novelty of who or what I've appropriated."

In an interview with *Guitar World*, Trent summed up his production philosophy. "I look at things differently than someone like Steve Albini, who seems to think that the point of the studio is to record a band efficiently with no frills, in its truest and most honest sense. I don't think anything's wrong with that, but at the same time I'm looking at the studio as a tool; why not use it? The challenge for me is not to go so overboard that the music becomes soulless and overproduced. I'd rather retain some sort of humanity amidst machinery."

Still, Reznor was happy to stick with the options offered by technology, allowing him to process, manipulate and reshape parts and performances rather than limiting himself to what can be achieved through real-time playing. "It's a great way to work. I don't really mind that most people shy away from that stuff, because that just gives me an edge over some guy who's too close-minded to accept that technology exists. He'll get a cable-ready television set, but he won't get a DAT machine because 'Ooooh, that's digital recording. I heard Neil Young say that doesn't sound good.' Like Neil Young would know his ass from a hole in the ground about digital recording. Nothing against Neil Young, but people get these archaic notions. . . .

"It ties in with a fear of change, which has brought about this current wave of retro—whether it be seventies disco or Pearl Jam, which to me just sounds like a seventies rock band. Or Lenny fucking Kravitz. . . . That whole mentality of 'real rock' and 'back to our roots,' or 'let's get back to what's safe—to be a real band like the Who or Rolling Stones, with two guitars, bass and drums.' Some people find entering a new technological era kind of scary and think, 'Let's go back to what we liked when we were kids.' But when we were kids everyone thought Queen and Kiss were terrible. Now they're a point of reference."

Despite Reznor's extensive use of technology, accident still plays a prominent role in Nine Inch Nails's recording process. "I luck into things," he says. "I think that due to laziness—not coming back and fixing things—they end up becoming more interesting. My instinct is to repair, edit. But then I'll get so used to hearing it, (so) I'll end up leaving it alone.

"I'll do a few twenty- or twenty-five-minute sessions of me just playing guitar. Then I'll listen back to it and say, 'Around ten minutes in I did something cool.' I'll cut that section out and put it aside. I'll cut maybe twenty parts out that way and put each one in the right space. It's not so much avoiding having to play the whole song as it is a tool to flesh out an arrangement."

Often, he says, he'll "take parts that were played fairly sloppy and loop it so that it repeats maybe every bar. The looping gives it a weird kind of precision, yet the looseness of the playing makes it sound a little 'off.' You'd have a very hard time achieving that kind of result just by playing a keyboard into a sequencer. So, 99 percent of the stuff we do—even vocals—is recorded into the computer first. We get an arrangement together and then dump it to tape."

Unlike most guitar players, Reznor's not one to engage in long conversations about gear. "Almost everything was direct. There was almost no miking of cabinets. I just don't like that sound very much. It sounds boring to me.

"A lot of the sounds on 'Mr. Self Destruct' that seem like guitar performances that no human being ever played are actually real performances that have been processed to unknown depths using Turbo Synth. Another thing I'll sometimes do is play the guitars twice as fast as the song's tempo, recording them at thirty ips (inches per second) on the multitrack. Then I'll slow it down to fifteen ips. I'll play the part an octave high too, so when I slow it down, it's in the right register and at the right speed. But if you saturate the tape real hard when you record it at thirty ips, it takes on a really clear, thick, warm and bizarre quality when you slow it down. The guitar on (the *Broken* version of) 'Suck'—which I think is the best guitar sound I've ever gotten—was done that way."

During Reznor and crew's stay at Le Pig, the house also played host to the first outside act to sign with Reznor's new Nothing label, the Florida glam-goth quintet Marilyn Manson, which recorded a few tracks for its debut album *Portrait of an American Family* there with Reznor, who said that recording on the site of the Manson murders was "something they had wanted to do for a long time."

Another visitor to the house was L.A.-based singer/songwriter Tori Amos, who during some of the project's darker stages would visit and offer encouragement to the depressed Reznor. On one occasion, according to Reznor, Amos attempted to cook him a chicken dinner but apparently the house's restless spirits had other ideas. Trent claims that even after six hours in the oven, the chicken was still bloody and raw.

Reznor and Amos became friends through a mutual admiration for each other's work. She later invited Trent to contribute a guest vocal to the song "Past the Mission" on her 1994 album *Under the Pink*. "We met on a friendship level; it was not like some mutual ass-kissing thing," he told *Axcess*. I really liked her first album, which is not the kind of thing I'd normally listen to. Someone had given it to me and said that it sounded like Sinead O'Connor. I fucking can't stand Sinead O'Connor, so I ignored it. Then I saw the video for 'Silent All These Years' and it struck me in a way where I wasn't sure if I liked it or not. But it was interesting. I was pleasantly surprised to find someone who I thought was taking chances. Not playing it safe, and also writing good songs, melodies and really good lyrics . . . I relate to her work a lot, on some level . . . She approaches things with a totally different aesthetic than I do, but it's good."

CHAPTER 12

Trent and company in attack mode
(© Jay Blakesberg, Retna Ltd.)

Dawn of the dread (© Adrian Boot, Retna Ltd.)

Trent and onetime bandmate/best pal Rich Patrick, in pre-feud days
(© Neal Preston, Retna Ltd.)

Onstage at Woodstock II: a baptism in mud
(Neal Preston, Retna Ltd. © A & M records)

Robin Finck in a not-at-all sinister pose
(© Stills / Retna Ltd., 70 rue Jean Bleuzen 92170 Vanves, France)

Rage incarnate (© Eddie Malluk / Retna Ltd.)

Suffering for his art on the cross of commerce

Offstage and inscrutable
(© Steve Eichner, Retna Ltd.)

The Thin White Duke meets the King of Pain
(© Jay Blakesberg / Retna Ltd.)

The Tate house was demolished shortly after *The Downward Spiral* was finished; Trent reportedly kept the front door as a souvenir. Meanwhile, the musical fruit of his stint at Le Pig justified the pain of its birthing process.

Indeed, the album was Nine Inch Nails's most musically powerful and emotionally cohesive effort yet, boasting a broad range of inventive noise manipulations, unexpected rhythmic shifts and memorable melodic hooks alongside Reznor's most bravely personal set of lyrics yet.

Though the music was less overtly guitar-dominated then *Broken*, guitar remained a prominent element on *The Downward Spiral*, with the instrument often taking on unexpected new sounds and shapes thanks to the artist's restless computer manipulations, which ironically were often used to make the music sound more organic and less mechanical.

"On *Downward Spiral*, I got to explore making an electronic record that doesn't sound electronic for some parts of it," Trent told *Spin*. "We did things with drums that I don't know if anyone has really done. We sampled drums in stereo with stereo mics and discovered if you play them on keyboard it sounds like you're sitting behind the drums for real. On 'March of the Pigs,' 'Eraser' and those songs, there's no live drums, but it alluded to being real because it didn't sound like a machine. No way someone could play that like that. It further added a kind of mindfuck to it. Instead of falling into a Ministry-type trap of how can I make things harder and harder, it's scarier to have something creep up on you."

True to the album's title, the songs chronicle a willing descent into self-destruction, via sex, drugs, violence and suicide. "The big overview was of somebody who systematically throws away every aspect of his life and what's around him, from personal relationships to religion," Reznor explained to *Guitar World*. "This person is giving up to a certain degree, but also finding some peace by getting rid of things that were bogging him down. The record also looks at certain vices as being ways of trying to dull the pain of what this person is hiding. Of course I'm talking about myself. So that was the general theme. Not that that's any great leap for me, thematically. The reason why I hope people like Nine Inch Nails is the lyrics. I think that's the element I care about most on this record, in terms of honesty and nakedness of emotion."

Where *Pretty Hate Machine* railed against an abstract, amorphous system and *Broken* submerged itself in all-consuming rage, on *The Downward Spiral* things were considerably less black and white. But the songs consistently returned to Reznor's favorite theme, control, which he addresses in a variety of guises.

"The three records have different focal points, or viewpoints," Trent explained to *Spin*. "*Broken's* central theme is self-loathing; on *Downward Spiral* I'm searching for some kind of self-awareness; and on *Pretty Hate Machine* I'm depressed by everything around me, but I still like myself. I've still got myself. On *Broken*, I've lost myself; nothing's better, and I want to die. *Downward Spiral* was searching for the core, by stripping away all the different layers."

The songs' running order, according to Reznor, "was made to work as a climax and then go down a tube," eventually descending into images of paranoia, murder and finally suicide. Meanwhile, the individual tracks embraced a variety of sonic approaches as broad as the emotional themes explored in the songs' lyrics.

The opening track, "Mr. Self Destruct," sets the tone for the album with a jagged, uneasy techno-thrash assault as Reznor screams "I am the voice inside your head and I control you." It's followed by the slinky, subdued "Piggy," the icily electronic "Heresy" and the furiously metallic "March of the Pigs."

"Heresy"—with the lyric hook "God is dead and no one cares"—compellingly mixes themes of sex and religion. According to Reznor, "I was trying to explore some of the paranoia I have as a sexually active person in the age of AIDS. I guess I feel cheated for not growing up in a more liberated era. At the same time, what gets me mad is the way the right wing has used the 'convenience' of this epidemic in helping to promote their own agenda."

Reznor says that the recurring pig imagery on the album is mainly a coincidence and not intended as a reference to the Manson murders. "I had the song 'Piggy' written long before it was ever known that I would be in that house. 'March of the Pigs' has nothing to do with the Tate murders or anything like that. I'm not going to say what it is about, but it's not about that."

He terrifyingly enters a killer's psyche on "Piggy," delivering the disquieting statement "Nothing can stop me now, 'cause I don't care" in a whispery vocal that conveys more evil than any shout could. "March of the Pigs—" apparently inspired by the torment of animals on their way to slaughter—featured an unexpectedly sweet piano hook that gently but firmly broke through the song's layers of feedback-laden terror.

The groove-laden "Closer" is simultaneously the album's most accessible pop song and its most subversive move, undercutting its majestic infectiousness with lyrics of self-hatred and sexual obsession, crystallized in the decidedly non-airplay-friendly chorus "I want to fuck you like an animal."

"I was trying to get a vibe something like the song 'Nightclubbing,' from Iggy Pop's album *The Idiot*. I don't know what it sounded like when it came out, but now it sounds like a real obvious, cheesy, almost disco, song—but in a cool way. I actually sampled the drums off that song to get a totally bad-sounding electronic drum effect. When I started doing that and the Prince-like harmonies on the verse I thought, 'How am I going to be able to do this? I'm supposed to be tough. I gotta act tough.' But I'm having fun doing it, so I'm gonna do it. It's scarier to do that than to do 'Self Destruct'-type songs. You try to do something light or bordering on a forbidden genre of music, like dance music . . .

"I think the idea of shocking somebody is a device that can be tastefully used. Even in a song like 'Closer.' Kick into the chorus and it says 'fuck' right the first thing. The first time you hear that you're not expecting that to pop in like that. And that in itself is a degree of shock. I'm not saying you're gonna jump out a window, but it's still a device to make you listen."

Having apparently learned that a whisper can be more effective than a scream in the right situation, Reznor also balanced the album's dark nihilism with moments of peaceful calm. Most obvious of these was the instrumental "A Warm Place," which, unlike most everything else in the NIN catalogue, hints at the potential of redemption. "I wanted to make a little spot in the context of the record where there was a break in the action," Trent explained to *Musician*. "In the midst of this buildup of these ever-growing, terrible machines, I just wanted to remember that there is somewhere . . . else."

No need to worry, though, as "A Warm Place" is followed by 'Eraser,' on which Reznor intones a pain-struck mantra over an ominous synth drone and an insistent drum beat.

Perhaps the album's most emotionally-draining track is the title number, whose lyrics Reznor wrote during a particularly fierce period of suicidal depression. The song has been described as the aural equivalent of a suicide note. "I had some reservations about (that song) being on there," he confessed to *Request*. "I realize that I may have to go on trial one day if someone kills themselves with it around. Is it the most responsible thing to say? No, but I'm not saying to go do it . . . I think the worst thing in the world would be someone hearing this record as an endorsement of suicide. It is absolutely not that; it's a moment that worked in the context of the story being told on the record. I have a degree of discomfort about it, just like I have a degree about saying, 'Kill me' (in the coda of "Eraser") on a record. There are a lot of insane people out there."

Following that song's decidedly bleak sentiments, *The Downward Spiral* closes with a suggestion of optimism in "Hurt," which addresses the pointless escapism of drug use with a harsh frankness that ultimately suggests the persistence of hope.

"With this record, I'm exploring subject matter that's not real uplifting, and some people will say, 'Oh, you're so depressed, don't you ever feel happy?' Of course I feel happy, but it's like if I was a director, and I was directing a movie about some heavy, sad topic. At the same time, Nine Inch Nails is a pretty accurate reflection of how I feet at the moment. If next week, I was to get married and feel completely happy and calm and placid, then it's time to stop the band or take a different direction.

"I think the very act of wanting to discover and uncover unpleasantries is itself positive. The act of trying to rid yourself of these demons, to prepare yourself for the worst, is a positive thing.

"I've never written an outright happy song," Reznor told U. magazine. "If I did, then I doubt it would fit into the context of a NIN record. And I don't really feel inspired to write about happy shit anyway. When I'm happy, the last thing I feel like doing is torturing myself with my notebook in hand.

"I am not trying to just bitch, or say that the world sucks," Reznor told *Plazm*. "I don't see any point in doing that. But I am trying to come to terms with my own head in a world that is chaotic and doesn't make sense. I'm trying to deal with my own thoughts and recycle them into something that I feel better about myself by expressing. And then, if someone says, 'I know what you're talking about, I feel the same way.' That's the best . . . You can't get a better compliment than that. And that's when it was worth sitting in that studio, or fighting with our lighting director, or doing interviews every day. That is the best reward. I'm a public servant.

"I think that this record and *Broken* work together interestingly, because there was no touring between," Trent told *Axcess*. "I finished one and basically started up on the next one without delay. *Broken* wasn't physically easy to make, but direction-wise, I knew what I wanted. This record had a less clear-cut path. I wanted to make something that wasn't just hard songs."

He also resisted the notion that the chaotically funky, witheringly bitter "Ruiner" was a return to *Broken*'s music-industry-rant mode. "That's not what I wrote it about," he told *Guitar World*. "But it could apply to that. I often don't consciously write about one particular thing. But then I realize, 'That's a perfect metaphor for what is happening with TVT,' or some other situation. But I don't set out to write songs about record labels. Nothing could be more boring—with the possible exception of writing about tour buses."

"Ruiner" was the song on the album that Reznor found hardest to get right. "There's always one song per record—maybe two if you're *real* lucky—where you work and work and work, and it just takes a hell of a long time for the song to come together. On *Pretty Hate Machine*, it was 'Kinda I Want To,' which I still think sucks, and 'That's What I Get.' Those songs took an unbelievable amount of work. Then you get into the trap of saying, 'Well, I spent so much time on this, it's gotta be good. I've *gotta* make it work.' It's usually one part that's fucking the whole thing up. And that's usually the part that you think is really great. You'll hear a million playbacks of the song and say, 'Man, that part is so fucking cool. Why is the song not happening?' Then finally someone hits the mute button for that part and the song's good. And you realize, 'Oh fuck, it's that part I love so much.' "

Despite *The Downward Spiral*'s unflinchingly intimate focus, the songs weren't strictly autobiographical. A friend of Trent's had recently watched his girlfriend shoot herself. And Lollapalooza-era NIN drummer Jeff Ward, despondent over his inability to kick a heroin habit, had committed suicide via carbon-monoxide poisoning. Indeed, the last line of the album's credits reads "We miss you Jeff Ward."

CHAPTER 13

The Downward Spiral, released in March 1994, was an instant smash, entering the *Billboard* charts at Number Two—undoubtedly the least commercial recording to ever make such a showing. But this sort of instant acceptance was by no means a foregone conclusion.

"The first people who heard it outside my immediate camp thought the album was commercial suicide," noted Reznor. "I'm not doing music to make millions of dollars, though. Every record I've put out I thought was risky at the time.

"My main goal was to broaden the scope of Nine Inch Nails a little bit. I'm tired of trying to second-guess what other people are going to like. It may not be the most obvious career move for me, but if you give the album a chance, it may produce something for you that you didn't expect.

"One of the main questions that plagued me as I was working was, 'Is this any good at all?' " Trent told *Request* on the eve of the album's release. "I'm not really sure. I think I've taken a chance. I've had a couple of people say, 'I like this, but I don't think the general public will.' I know what (they) mean."

He also credited Interscope for allowing him creative carte blanche, despite his numerous missed deadlines. "We've never really had any pressure from the record company," he told *RIP.* "When I delivered that record, it was the record I wanted to make and I felt it was artistically where I was at the time. I did have a bit of reservation, just because I thought it was commercially limited and I thought there wasn't many singles on there, if any. I obviously didn't care, 'cause I released it anyway.

"The nature of the music business is competitive," he acknowledged. "You're trying to make your product succeed in ways that other people's don't. In some ways, I found myself getting caught up in that and then I thought, 'What the fuck? This is the record that I like and I wanted to make. I've made it, here it is.' And it debuted that high on the charts and took everybody by surprise. And then you find yourself getting sucked back into that game of, 'Okay, what's the next single going to be? Is MTV going to play the video for this?' "

One of the most unexpected aspects of *The Downward Spiral*'s success was its widespread acceptance amongst mainstream music critics. As *New York Times* critic Jon Pareles observed, "The album is a series of songs about suicide and madness that contrasts the pointlessness of life and the reality of pain. This internalized anger is something Nine Inch Nails shares with bands like Nirvana. But, where Nirvana struck a chord by lashing out at the world of conformity, sexism and shattered hippie ideals that produced its generation's neuroses and dysfunctionalism, Nine Inch Nails's rage is more generalized, bemoaning not the futility of a generation but of existence itself."

In the May 1994 issue of *Playboy*, Vic Garbarini wrote, "Imagine the ferocity of a Nirvana guitar attack set in the cyberspace of early Pink Floyd, while a crazed tribe to John Bonham pounds out a thundering Led Zep-style drum frenzy. What's truly amazing is that as Reznor so ingeniously processes all this stuff through a bank of keyboard samplers and computers, you'd swear this was live music played by superhumans. . . . Although his lyrics are unremittingly bleak, Reznor is no Satan with a synth. He rails at the heavens in ways that will make you squirm, but there's something uplifting about it."

People magazine's Peter Castro gave *The Downward Spiral* an "A" and commented, "It's hard to imagine how an album that sounds as if it were recorded on an active airport runway could be captivating, but that's what this disc loudly achieves."

Writing in the April 1994 issue of *Time* magazine, critic Guy Garcia commented, "This is not music for the squeamish, or even the optimistic. Meshing the angry nihilism of punk and heavy metal with the synthetic sheen of techno, *The Downward Spiral* is a fourteen-song, sixty-five-minute howl of somebody falling into the void. What keeps it from being just another nauseating exercise in shock rock is the intelligence and creative force behind its dire sound."

Rolling Stone reviewer Jonathan Gold agreed that much of the album's effectiveness lay in Trent's newfound ability to temper his anger with other, more introspective moods. "Reznor's voice seduces and insinuates where it previously expressed itself only in animal screams," wrote Gold. "It slithers into your ears and curls up somewhere near the medulla oblongata. He sometimes even expresses an emotion that isn't anger, which throws the full-on assaults of his catch phrases—'Don't you tell me how I feel'; 'Your God is dead, and no one cares'—into brilliant relief."

Musician commented, "One listen to *The Downward Spiral* will change the way you think about electronic and industrial music forever. Combining technique and institution, Reznor has made machine music which carries the human pulse in ways that astonish. . . . But Reznor is not Lucifer with a drum machine; he's more like the suffering Job crossed with the raging Jeremiah, tearing down the false in a desperate, oddly confident search for higher reconciling truths."

Still, a few critics remained content to stick with one-dimensional blanket dismissals. For example, *Stereo Review* consigned *The Downward Spiral* to its list of the Ten Worst Pop Albums of 1994 with a flippant "What am I hearing here that my own garbage disposal can't tell me?"

By this point, Nine Inch Nails had become such a popular presence on MTV that video had emerged as a crucial component of NIN's creative life and of its relationship with its audience. But that didn't mean that NIN videos had an easier time getting on MTV with their contents intact.

Though at one point Reznor said that he had discussed the possibility of making a *Downward Spiral* long-form film/video project with provocative British film-maker Derek Jarman, the album eventually reached the video medium a series of individual song clips. While the largely unseen *Broken*-era videos were the product of Reznor's reckless embrace of visual extremes, 1994 found him in a somewhat more accessible frame of mind.

"The approach on this record was to work in the context of something that could be seen. I don't foresee four videos of reconstructive penis surgery. I think it's more challenging to work with something that's more accessible yet is interesting, different, subversive. I don't direct videos, so it's a challenge just to hook up with the right people. Work with more mainstream video directors, but take them out of context and experiment. (In the past) I found all people that hadn't done videos before with mixed results and it ended up being a lot of handholding. I don't have time for that right now."

"March of the Pigs" was actually shot twice, first in an unsuccessful, unreleased version and subsequently in a more successful visualization directed by Peter Christopherson. "The first one didn't work out due to my fault, conceptually," Trent said. "It was average. I wouldn't put out a record like that so why put out a video?"

The Germanically creepy clip for "Closer," directed by Madonna/R.E.M./Michael Jackson veteran Mark Romanek and partially shot on vintage 1920s film stock, was loaded with indelibly disturbing imagery, from crucified monkeys to Reznor himself spinning violently in midair. The "Closer" video only made it into heavy rotation after Reznor agreed to edit out some of its more jarring images, the edited version slyly added a "scene missing" card in place of the excised shots.

"I thought, fuck it, instead of the Super-8 video directors we've used in the past, underground people, let's go with Mr. Fucking Gloss, Mark Romanek, who just did that Michael Jackson piece of shit," Reznor told Spin. "So we decided to spend some money and go to ridiculous lengths to recreate works of artists we liked, from Joel-

Peter Witkin to Man Ray, Brothers Quay, this hodgepodge of stuff. That video was great, it was cool as fuck-looking. Right away, MTV said, 'Can't have that, can't have that.' Now okay, there was naked pussy. We knew that was going to get cut. And then we got complaints that people still found the video disturbing. 'Well, why?' 'Well, we don't know why, but it seems satanic and evil.' And then I thought, great, we did it."

Meanwhile, the artist continued to express reservations about the stardom he'd fought so hard to achieve. On the Downward Spiral track "I Do Not Want This"—on which he sang, "I just want to do something that matters"—Reznor hinted that he had begun to entertain the possibility that Nine Inch Nails may have grown beyond his control.

"I feel that way sometimes in fits of desperation and frustration," he said. "I want to make some impact, whether it's being a star or shooting a president or having a successful relationship with someone. I'm not sure what I want to do, but I want to matter to some degree to someone, or to myself.

"You know, I feel fortunate to be able to do what I do, but I don't feel content like I would if I'd surrounded myself with a bunch of good friends in a good situation in a place I like to be. The biggest revelation I've had about my own life is that I've done everything I've wanted to do and I'm still pretty miserable."

CHAPTER 14

Nine Inch Nails's commercial success had given Trent Reznor enough music industry clout to indulge his interests in other, less visible musical activities. For one thing, he found his services as a producer and remixer suddenly in demand, and was even offered a production deal by Sire Records.

But for the most part, Trent preferred to exercise his behind-the-scenes talents through Nothing Records, the label that he and John Malm were allowed to set up as part of NIN's deal with Interscope.

Though *Broken* bore the Nothing logo in 1992, the label didn't really get up and running as a going concern until the beginning of 1994, when it officially opened its doors and set about assembling a roster of acts.

"All you can do with a guy like Trent is to believe in him and let him go," Interscope chief Jimmy Iovine commented on Interscope's support for the new label. "No matter how odd what he's doing may look to us now, it will all seem exactly right in a year or so."

As of this writing, Nothing's biggest success has been slapstick-outrage specialists Marilyn Manson, whose Reznor-produced albums *Portrait of An American Family* and *Antichrist Superstar* were both NIN-style crossover smashes. If the label's other acts have yet to achieve similar sales levels, Nothing's releases have shown a consistent level of integrity and adventurousness, and the label has earned acclaim both for its musical vision and its innovative A&R approach.

Both Reznor and Malm have long maintained that

one of Nothing's fundamental goals was to give its artists a greater degree of control over their own work. "It was always a dream of ours to someday start a label," Malm told one interviewer. We wanted to set up a label in which artists are treated the way we felt we should have liked to have been treated. Essentially, if you sign somebody because they're a creative person, then let them do what they do instead of trying to change or mutate them.

"Trent and I have been partners since day one," Malm continued. "We went through the whole TVT thing together. After that unfortunate experience we always said that if we ever started our own label, we'd definitely know how to treat the artists—the way we wanted to be treated ourselves, and never were. Then Interscope entered the picture and we suddenly had that opportunity, which has since become Nothing, and with it our philosophy carried over—to sign true artists, let them do what they do, and don't interfere with how they do it. If they want our help, we're more than happy to give it. If they don't, we're more than happy to stand back and let them do their thing."

With headquarters in Lemko Hall, the plushest building in the gentrifying Tremont section of Cleveland (where Reznor once shared a cheap apartment with Chris Vrenna), Nothing is a relatively compact, streamlined operation, a reflection of Reznor and Malm's desire to keep the label small enough to be manageable. "It takes a lot of time, and I don't want to get to where I don't know what's going on," Reznor stated. "It's nice being able to do this and it's fun to put some energy into something other that Nine Inch Nails all the time."

In much the same way that Nine Inch Nails delivers finished records to Interscope without standard A&R interference, Nothing is given a similarly free hand to deliver its releases to the parent company, which in turn releases what Nothing gives them.

"I feel that NIN is in a pretty fortunate position with Interscope," said Reznor. "They have enough faith in me as an artist, that if I say, 'Hey, I wanna do this video, and I wanna do this, and I wanna make a record, go on tour and lose money' . . . they think, 'There must be some reason to this. Okay, we don't understand it, but we'll let you do it.' And they do, and then I think at the end of the day they realize what the master plan was. I like working that way because if I get an idea, I can execute it. I don't have to have it approved by fifteen people whose opinions I don't respect anyway. To be able to offer a version of that type of situation to other bands, that makes me feel good.

"It's basically just to provide a shell to other bands to have a concrete environment," Reznor told *Huh*. "And also to be aware of how the business part of it works—which most labels don't want artists to know. There's so much shit in the music business aimed at protecting the label and fucking the artist over. I've learned 'cause I've gotten fucked, and there's no reason it should be that way. Everybody assumes you're gonna fuck them over so they fuck you over first. It's stupid."

Nothing's signing policies genuinely do seem based

on Reznor and Malm's personal tastes rather than commercial expediencies. "When this idea of a label came around, honestly, I had been wanting to help out Marilyn Manson in some way," says Trent. "A couple of major labels had been dragging their feet with them, and I thought of them as a perfect example of a band that I thought really had a good vision. They had a unique stance, something to say, good songs to back it up with, and they were good musicians. In the wrong hands, that could be shaped into something that was very mediocre . . . If they smooth off a rough edge here, take that lyric out of here and don't do that on stage there, pretty soon it's not the true thing anymore."

"Trent gives us full artistic freedom, the kind of freedom no other label would even consider giving a band," agreed Marilyn Manson's namesake lead singer. And if any band seemed likely to test the limits of limits tolerance, it's Marilyn Manson, a cartoonishly violent hard-rock outfit that's been described as a more malevolent Twisted Sister. The Florida quintet—whose members all use stage names combining the first names of female sex symbols and the surnames of mass murderers—courted controversy from the start, with songs about murder, kinky sex and child molestation prominently featured on their debut album.

Even the permissive Interscope initially balked at releasing *Portrait of An American Family*. Reznor: "Interscope said, 'Well, we don't think we can release this 'cause it's offensive to us. Would you consider . . . ' 'No. I will not change a fucking thing on that record. If you don't wanna put it out, then we'll shop it to someone else.' Then they realized it was kinda silly. I personally don't find it offensive at all. I don't think rock should be safe anyway. If there's something offensive about it, then good, there's not enough of that today, in my opinion."

Almost immediately upon the album's release in the summer of 1994, Marilyn Manson met with outraged resistance from society's moral hall monitors. The album was even pulled from numerous stores in Britain after a member of Parliament publicly branded it "an outrage against society."

In addition to giving Nothing its first sales success, Marilyn Manson's glam-goth hard rock also freed the company from an unwanted image as an "industrial" label. "We're just looking for interesting stuff," states Malm. "A lot of artists get their own labels, and most of them fall by the wayside. But we're really taking things seriously; we'd like to be around in ten or twenty years."

Other acts on the Nothing roster include the influential British trio Coil, whose eerily textured melancholy made them a Reznor favorite, and whose keyboardist Peter Christopherson has directed several videos and done a number of remixes for NIN; eclectic British dance-pop act Pop Will Eat Itself, who ply a good-humored mix of tribal dance-pop, trance atmospherics, rock punch and cyber imagery; influential U.K. industrialists Meat Beat Manifesto, who'd toured with NIN circa *Pretty Hate Machine*; the Cleveland-based Prick, a.k.a. Reznor's old Cleveland friend and Lucky Pierre bandmate Kevin McMahon, whose self-titled debut album employed an array of sonic moods, from metallic noise to lush orchestrations to riffy rock; and the familiarly named Pig, the studio brainchild of KMDFM founder Raymond Watts. More surprising, perhaps, is Nothing's signing of former Judas Priest frontman Rob Halford.

When asked by *Axcess* what qualities he looked for in a potential Nothing act, Reznor answered, "A sense of originality. Having something to say, not being caught up in following the trend of the moment. Some sort of uniqueness that needs to be heard. And that uniqueness is the thing that I think is the most important and needs to be protected from meddling major labels. They tend to soften the edges to get it on the radio or to imitate whoever's at the top of the charts. And I think that most of what's on MTV right now is terrible. Radio I don't much like either. Why is that? Is it that human beings just aren't making interesting music anymore?"

As evidenced by his label's stable of acts, Reznor obviously doesn't believe that's the case.

CHAPTER 15

In the wake of *The Downward Spiral*'s instant left-field success, Nine Inch Nails returned to the road, undertaking its most extensive and ambitious tour to date. Still, Reznor admitted to having mixed emotions about touring, an activity that had occupied a major chunk of his life during the past few years.

"I have a certain degree of newfound maturity," he told *U.* magazine, "and it makes me desire some kind of permanence like having a home. But now I'm faced with getting on a tour bus for at least a year. And as great as that can be, it's ultimately a rather shallow existence."

He admitted to *Spin* that tales of on-the-road debauchery in the NIN camp have some basis in fact. "When I get off the road, I'm not good at making tons of friends. I'm not great at entertaining people. When I'm doing a record, I don't ever go out. The real me gets up at a regular kind of schedule, writes music and doesn't party all the time. On the road I adopt a certain kind of mentality. A lot of it is juvenile, but it's also about staying sane in an insane situation.

"It's politically incorrect these days in the alternative world to indulge and have fun in a touring situation. Certain camps like to say we're a horrible, ridiculous throwback to cock-rock bullshit. That's not what we're about. But at the same time, if there's fun to be had, why not? Nobody gets hurt. And I'm not going to be doing this forever."

To translate the new album to the concert stage, Reznor assembled a new live band, with Chris Vrenna back on drums, Lollapalooza-era keyboardist James Wool- **145** ley, and new recruits Robin Finck and Danny Lohner. The two newcomers divvied up guitar, bass and keyboard duties.

"I set up the framework and I explain to them what Nine Inch Nails is all about," Trent said of his relationship with his subordinate bandmates. "I'm pretty heavy-handed at first, to make sure everyone understands what we're trying to be. It's not about playing perfect every night. It's about just understanding the message of the songs, whatever they might mean to you. And getting that point across. That speaks a lot louder than a cool haircut or a virtuoso guitar solo. I think the guys I've got are good players. But I didn't get them because they were the best players. (I got them because) they had an understanding of what I was trying to say. Once I saw they were getting it, then it was, 'Okay, now make it your own.' Live, we don't sound like the record. I don't care, I don't want to sound like the record."

"Usually we find out what's going on with Nine Inch Nails by reading Trent's interviews in magazines," James Woolley confided to *Rolling Stone*. "I think he likes the band now, but I guess we're all still a little too nervous to ask him."

Nine Inch Nails's Self-Destruct tour unveiled the band's most elaborate live experience to date. Early on in the tour, Reznor, ever the perfectionist control freak, spent two days personally reprogramming the computer software controlling the stage lighting. "It was looking like a Genesis concert," he said at the time. "Somebody had to get the job done."

Not much else on the Self-Destruct tour seemed likely to remind fans of Genesis. Certainly not the rubber fetish stage backdrop that remained all but invisible to most of the crowd through the show thanks to the copious amounts of onstage fog, or the banks of harsh lights and endless layers of unruly electronic noise that often drowned out many of the real instruments.

But the band's most compelling special effect was, as always, Reznor himself, manically prowling the stage, smashing gear (by now the band could afford to bring along a crew member whose job it was to repair the instruments that Reznor regularly pummeled onstage) and howling like rage incarnate.

"I'm not trying to hide, or make up for a lack of songs, but essentially Nine Inch Nails are theater," Reznor told *Rolling Stone*. "What we do is closer to Alice Cooper than Pearl Jam."

Still, he staunchly resisted the implication that the theatricality of NIN's stage presentation somehow negates its realness. "I'm afraid some of this stuff is pretty intense, and I can see how it can be dismissed as calculating and theatrical," he told *Musician*. "But it's real to me."

The Self-Destruct tour found Nine Inch Nails introducing another new element to their live presentation: musical subtlety. As on the album, the heavier excesses were balanced by quieter, more contemplative moments that provided a heartfelt respite from the overall chaos and provided an effective counterpoint to the show's more violent elements.

Reviewing NIN's May 17 show at New York's Webster Hall, *New York Times* critic Jon Pareles noted, "Reznor is among the very few musicians who brings together both current dance music, which is largely keyboard-driven, and hard rock, which worships guitars. In fact, he borrows widely, taking ideas from Brian Eno's ambient keyboard music, Slayer's jackhammer guitars, Ministry's caustic keyboard samples and the somber blasphemies of Depeche Mode. Yet with all their obvious antecedents, the songs don't sound like pastiches. The fusion brings vehement nihilism to a broad audience."

Pareles further noted the gap between NIN's recorded sound and the band's live approach. "Instead of the ominous electronic soundscapes Mr. Reznor creates on his albums, the band comes up with precisely plotted blunt assaults. Reznor knows how to use slow crescendos, and sudden quiet patches, to make loud passages sound even more vociferous."

Describing Reznor's stage persona, Pareles continued, "He performed in designer tatters, often in near darkness despite batteries of strobe lights, with his body hunched over and his face contorted: an image of powerless agony, not the conquering belligerence of heavy metal. The music, plotted for drama and impact, comes across as both desperate and vengeful. The singer may be backed into a corner by brutal authority figures and his own inchoate fears, but as he snarled in the set's final song, 'I'd rather die than give you control.' "

CHAPTER 16

Nine Inch Nails's appearance at the twenty-fifth-anniversary Woodstock festival in August of 1994 proved to be another turning point in the band's career. Much as the Lollapalooza tour had three years earlier, the band's Woodstock appearance signalled another jump in NIN's public profile and commercial status. At the same time, NIN's presence at the festival seemed to embody the event's unintentionally ironic juxtaposition of sunny idealism and hard-headed capitalism.

But if Woodstock II signalled NIN's arrival as a major act, Trent claimed that it was never intended to be a milestone. He freely admitted that he accepted the offer to play the festival mainly for the money, which would help offset the costs involved in staging the elaborate larger-venue shows that the band would soon be playing.

But a life-threatening crisis was in the cards before the band could play its Saturday-evening Woodstock set. After arriving on Friday night and sleeping on their tour bus, the band was abruptly wrested out of bed on Saturday morning. Reznor: "A power line had fallen on the bus and there was voltage going through the bus while we were on it. I went back to the bunks: 'Guys, don't panic, but try not to touch any metal. There is a lot of voltage going through the bus right now.' I walk to the front of the bus, and I see fucking Crosby, Stills and Nash looking in, and a sea of cameras, seeing me in my underpants . . ."

"People were screaming 'Don't touch anything metal! Don't get off the bus! Don't pee!' " Chris Vrenna told the *Milwaukee Journal*. "Everyone's staring at our bus and we're all in our underwear going, 'What's going on?' "

Reznor insists that the memorable image of the mud-encrusted musicians on the Woodstock stage wasn't a calculated ploy for attention, but the innocent result of backstage play prior to the band's set. As he told *RIP*, "We were right out by the big mud pit and watchin' everybody, I thought, 'Well, this looks like a lot of fun' . . . It was just a real nervous day. Then on the way to stage I pushed Danny, and he just fell face-first into the mud. Then he tackled me and it turned into a kind of all-male mud wrestling thing. After we did that, all nervousness kind of subsided."

Onstage, the mud mixed with sweat and made it difficult for Reznor to get through the set. "I'm still cleaning the mud out of my ears," he told *USA Today*. "I couldn't see. Every time I turned my head, my hair would slap mud in my eye. There was mud on the guitar strings. It wasn't conducive to technical greatness."

While Reznor insisted that the Nails's Woodstock performance was subpar due to the technical glitches inherent in playing such an event, it was impressive enough to lead many observers to proclaim that NIN had stolen the show from the array of popular contemporaries and legendary elders who shared the bill. With a live crowd of 350,000 and an additional pay-per-view television audience estimated at 250,000, there's no doubt that Woodstock did much to expand Nine Inch Nails's fan base. The festival, Trent told *Spin*, "was the most nerve-wracking day of my life. But that changed things for us a lot, in terms of brand-name recognition.

"I think that we've been branded safe and acceptable and I don't think any programmer's gonna get fired for playing a NIN song after the Woodstock thing," he said. "When we did Woodstock, I thought we would be, y'know, number twenty-five in the list of fifty bands that were playing there. When it kinda worked out that we've been getting a lot of attention from it, I never expected that. I don't exactly know why, 'cause I thought our performance was shitty."

On the heels of Woodstock, the "Closer" video became a fixture on MTV, *The Downward Spiral* began moving back up the sales charts and Trent achieved perhaps the ultimate in mainstream recognition for a musician—a cover story in that flagship of middle-of-the-road acceptance, *Rolling Stone*.

As he told RIP, " 'Closer' gets added at MTV, and somehow people at Woodstock think we did good, and somehow the timing of *Rolling Stone* finally offering us a cover (seemed) like it was all perfect-planned, which it's not. It seems like, 'Hey, flavor-of-the-moment,' and then there's a danger in that where you also become yesterday's news the next moment. I've been aware of that, and I've never had any desire to be 'heavy-rotation-MTV-boy' or anything else.

"I know when I go to sleep at night, I've made the record I wanna make, without any compromise. If that is a sellout, then I'm a hundred-percent sellout . . . I'm not going to go up to somebody and say, 'You live in Ohio, you shop in a mall, hey fuck you, you're not cool enough to listen to my music.' That's fuckin' facism. I was one of those kids. If people like it, great. If you don't like it, it's my fault too."

Another sign of Nine Inch Nails's new household-name status was that on the tour following Woodstock—which kicked off, appropriately enough, in Cleveland—the band became the target of fundamentalist Christian groups who judged Trent and company to be doing the devil's work. More than one show on the tour would feature protests from born-again picketers.

"Rock music was never meant to be safe," Reznor told the Los Angeles Times. "There needs to be an element of intrigue, mystery, subversiveness. Your parents should hate it. If you think I worship Satan because of something you see in the 'Closer' video, great!"

The next leg of the tour found the band playing arena-size venues with opening acts Marilyn Manson and the Jim Rose Circus Sideshow in tow. The arena shows featured a more grandiose stage presentation, including an elegantly draped backdrop, imposing onstage columns and banks of lights that would bathe the stage in various colors. During "Hurt," the band was largely obscured by a screen onto which was projected a montage of black-and-white images of death, decay and all manner of human atrocities. Reznor, dwarfed by the visuals, sang of feeling insignificant.

A high point of the tour was a sold-out two night stand at New York's Madison Square Garden, with the band bizarrely introduced by David Letterman sidekick Larry "Bud" Melman. As Jason Cohen observed in his Spin review of the December 9 Madison Square Garden show, "Bitch, bitch, bitch: That's the game Reznor excels at playing, albeit with considerable melodramatic sex-God-and-death flourish. But he's also a showman, despite his admission that he 'never thought Nine Inch Nails would be playing this fucking place.' Reznor's hyperathleticism and broadly aggressive gestures are made for the arena, and with one third of the floor set off as a pit, the audience is too, replacing the beach ball with the bodysurfer as they mosh before the show."

Cohen opined that, unlike the multi-tiered *Downward Spiral*, the band's live show offered a relatively one-dimensional view of NIN. "Live, Nine Inch Nails offers no tickles, caresses or climaxes, just relentless episodes of brutality. Reznor's flair for dark beauty and ornate pop craftsmanship is crushed by the wheels of industry, as his equally strong penchant for battering-ram percussion and ear-splitting chaos takes over completely. When Reznor sledgehammers his keyboard, it's hard to distinguish the crash from when he's actually playing the thing."

Reviewing the same Madison Square Garden show, *New York Times* critic Neil Strauss stated, "Reznor's music is almost identical to . . . Cabaret Voltaire, Ministry and Nitzer Ebb, who mixed industrial noise with disco beats. But none of these bands reached the audience that Mr. Reznor has, probably because Nine Inch Nails offers something they didn't—catharsis. Mr. Reznor laced his music with ripping heavy-metal power chords, tore apart the stage in choreographed fits of rage and made sure that the seats in the first third of the ground floor were removed so that the audience could slam-dance."

The Nine Inch Nails live experience even received a seal of approval from no less an authority than Adam Ant, who, with longtime guitar sidekick Marco Pirroni, joined Reznor and company on stage in New York and Worcester, Massachusetts, to perform "Physical," as well as two obscure Adam and the Ants numbers, "Red Scab" and "Beat My Guest," that the Nails had worked up for the occasion. Calling Nine Inch Nails "the scariest band on the planet," Ant commented, "it felt like the Marquee in '77, the way punk should have gone."

CHAPTER 17

By the end of 1994, the name of the Self-Destruct tour had gotten a bit too close for comfort. Just before Christmas, Reznor's golden retriever Maise—whom many close to Trent viewed as his last link to a "normal" life outside of Nine Inch Nails—was mortally wounded after falling from a third-floor balcony at a Columbus, Ohio, concert hall. In response, Reznor cancelled the next night's show and flew off to Miami to recuperate. According to witnesses, he then dove headlong into what he referred to as "Self-Destruct mode," submerging his pain in a whirlwind of indulgence.

Not long after, Reznor suffered an allergic reaction that caused a rash that covered most of his body. In his efforts to rid himself of it, he tried a variety of herbal remedies, bathed in a lavender/chamomile/peppermint concoction and even covered himself with clay.

When he wasn't battling his psychic demons or his allergies, Trent continued to wrestle with the contradictions inherent in his role as arena-level rock star, remaining skeptical of his own success while acknowledging the absurdity of complaining about the situation. His interviews during this period reveal a deep ambivalence about his current position as unlikely cultural icon.

"When I think about the state I'm in, I feel like a fucking loser because I've got things I really should be glad about," he told *Musician*. "I'm aware that I'm fortunate to live in this house and do what I've always wanted to do. And be one of the few who got the record deal. I hear myself bitching about how it sucks to be popular, **159** then I have to just stop because that's bullshit to say so. By the same token, I'm not more happy or content with my life than I was ten years ago. I got everything I wanted in my life . . . except I don't really have a life right now. I don't have any real friends, any relationships that mean anything to me, and I've turned myself into this music-creation-performance machine.

"Every day I'm saying the most personal thing I could ever say," he said to *Details*. "And I don't know if I want people in my head that much, but I've chosen to give that out because I realized that's what made the strongest statement, that was the most honest art I could make. But one of the prices is that there's an open raw nerve that I'm letting everybody look at. There's a hole in the back of my pants with a bare asshole showing, and you can see right in there. And sometimes I wish I hadn't."

He further told *Plazm*, "I meet people and they think they know me because they've read an interview with me or they've read lyrics—'Man, I know how you feel.' You might know *some* of how I feel. You see that a lot with the Kurt Cobain situation. 'What did he have to kill himself for? Blah blah blah' . . . When someone says, 'Hey man, what does he have to be sad about? He's a rich rock star . . . ' Someone who says that is someone who has never attained any goals that they've set for themselves. When you do, you start to realize that this is cool but it's not exactly like I'd dreamed. I'm not the most content person in the world just because someone bought my record. There is more to it than that."

By now, the intensity—and potential for physical danger—of the band's live shows had escalated to the point where Reznor quit his trademark stage-diving due to the numerous injuries he'd sustained. "Why do I not jump in the crowd? Because my shirt gets ripped off and someone sticks their finger in my butt."

Whatever his ambivalence about his life as a rock star, the Self-Destruct tour was a massive success, both artistically and commercially. "This band is so *big* now," Reznor said to *Huh*. "This tour has gotten bigger than anyone expected it to be and it's not . . . I'm not so comfortable. I had a lot more fun with the band playing clubs than I do with a forty person crew, where I don't know the names of half the guys on it.

"There's that weird juxtaposition of singing to audiences of being isolated and not being able to fit into anything or relate to anybody. To find a little niche you can just disappear into and be normal. To not have pain, and have the path laid out for you, which is something I long for at times. And you're onstage with 10,000 people grabbing at you, do you know what I mean? You're meaning what you're singing and looking down at these subhuman things going, take a shit on my head, spit on me, anything. That fucks up anybody after a while. I've learned these little ploys where when the audience isn't into it I'd ram it down their throats and get them to hate us."

Nagging contradictions aside, Reznor acknowledged the emotional payoff he still draws from a successful performance. "I absolutely feel that it's a positive release. Like, some of the songs hit home to where, this sounds idiotic, but honestly, tears just . . . 'Terrible Lie' is one that always kicks into gear. Maybe the first minute I'm adjusting to technically what's wrong onstage, the monitor is feeding back, but by the end of the song it's taken you over and you mean what you say. You can't fake that, people can tell. There's a feeling of elation and a strong sense of calmness. Suddenly, I don't really have a desire to go out and fight people anymore. I've gotten something out of my system, and when you do that four or five times a week for a couple of years that's enough.

"Often by the end of the show when the last thing you feel like doing is going onstage, and your throat's sore and at some point you look out on the crowd and they know the words and they're shouting them back at you, and they're having a real experience of flushing it out of their systems—it's probably the best feeling of my life."

CHAPTER 18

Whatever his personal and professional demons, Trent Reznor has always maintained an admirable ability to view his work—and his public persona—with a sense of objectivity. "I'm always a little bit depressed, and I should probably go to therapy," he told *Request*, adding slyly, "but that would ruin my career.

"I don't know or care, really, what people think about me," he told *MuchMusic*. "I'll read interviews of me where I'm portrayed as something that I know I don't think I am, if I know who I am anymore, but I don't care.

"Anytime I do things in the press, regardless of how I act, they're usually looking for something and they find it whether it was there or not," he told *RIP*. "If it was to portray me as X, Y or Z, if it was to portray me as king of the vampires or king of the pretentious assholes or whatever it might be, it doesn't really matter what I'm saying."

That's not to say that he completely turns the other cheek to criticism. "I wanna kill people who say this is a formula," he said to *USA Today*. "When I first did interviews, I considered pretending to be someone else. But I couldn't lie. I was embarrassed that I didn't have the barrier of a character, like Alice Cooper. I'm not proud to say I hate myself and don't like what I am.

"It's all basically me," he told *Guitar World*. "It's all my personality, but it's amplified in a certain direction. I get a lot of people saying, 'Wow, you must be the most depressed person in the world!' Well, I don't think I am. I'm **165** not the happiest guy in the world either. But when I'm writing songs, I deliberately try to explore incredibly black emotions—combining personal experience with imaginative projection—to see how far I can get. I often end up bumming myself out pretty good.

"The character on stage is an amplification of me, of the energy in me and my personality," he told Much-Music. "I don't walk around throwing mic stands when I'm eating dinner at a restaurant. But it's not an act, it was never conceived to be some persona that I . . . it is me, it's a different side of me."

The idea of pushing the envelope—in terms of both sonic and emotional content—had become something of a personal crusade for Reznor. "I have a bit of a chip on my shoulder," he admitted to Spin. "Maybe it's from being keyboard-oriented. Not that bringing the keyboard to the forefront is one of my main goals . . . The point is more to just bring people out of complacency. Sonically, lyrically—your parents should hate it. Bob Dole should have a fucking problem with it. That's what's best about what I'm told rock 'n' roll was, at one time. I could make music that I find interesting, that's experimental, instrumental noise records, and I may do that sometime. But I'm more interested, now that fate has dealt me the cards that people are interested in what I'm doing, to see how far I can push."

That agenda is all the more daring in a popular culture that often seems to encourage mediocrity. In such an environment, penetrating the mainstream pop consciousness with nonmainstream music and nonmainstream ideas is more subversive than ever. "I watch MTV because I am morbidly fascinated with how bad most of what I'm seeing is," says Trent. "Occasionally, something will sneak out that's all right. What I think could have been a unique new art form has become a series of three-minute commercials for products. This one might be for Bon Jovi and that one for Pearl Jam and that one for Close-Up tooth polish or whatever. It's interchangeable. Just look how corporate and unchallenging the whole genre of rock video has become. I think that someone realized a while ago that one channel that goes everywhere in the country is much more important than any radio station."

As he lamented to *Guitar World*, "Everything is so product-oriented now. I was never a great fan of vinyl, but it seems that around the time that vinyl died and CD came to life, the quality of music went way down. Around the same time MTV came into its own. And now there's very little that's genuinely dangerous, rebellious or exciting about rock.

"I think popular music sucks today," he told *Spin*. "For the most part, I cannot fucking stand the shit that's at the top of the charts. Now, I'm not saying my sole mission is to turn people on to other music. But maybe I can change things a bit."

Though he was obviously intrigued by the possibilities offered by his position as an influential media figure, Reznor also suggested, following the media blitz that accompanied both *The Downward Spiral* and the Self-Destruct tour, that it might be a good time to temporarily retreat from public scrutiny. "I'm uncomfortable enough reading anything that comes out of my mouth," he told *RIP*, "that I feel like enough has been said now, time to go away for a while."

Reznor's wariness of media overexposure is certainly understandable, as fame has brought with it all manner of personal intrusions, unfounded accusations and wild rumors. Reports of Trent's death have circulated at various times, as have equally inaccurate accusations that he is a former pal of cannibalistic mass-murderer Jeffrey Dahmer.

By this point, Reznor's image and musical style had become so recognizable—and exploitable—that a TV ad for Gatorade featured a Trent lookalike as well as a suspiciously familiar-sounding tune. "I had a hundred people say, 'Why did you do that Gatorade commercial?' I was like, 'What are you talking about?' I hadn't seen it. I finally got a copy. It was 'Down In It.' The beat's a little bit different. The singing has got a little bit of distortion, exactly the same kind of thing as my voice. So I looked into how we can sue these fuckheads. I don't want money. I just don't want them using my song."

Even after *The Downward Spiral* had reached multiplatinum status, Reznor continued to insist that NIN's commercial appeal carried built-in limitations. Nine Inch Nails, he claimed, "isn't the kind of band that can ever be a Pearl Jam. It's appealing to a limited cross-section of people. Pearl Jam, to me, are a good band at what they are and they're also all things to all people. They've managed to be labeled alternative, (but) their songs are already on classic rock stations. There's not one element of anything that they've ever done that would offend your grandmother, there's a cute guy in the band, it's teen-throb, it's alternative rock in theory, (but) it's corporate rock. They're on every chart. They're everything to all people. And they're politically-fuckin'-correct. Nine Inch Nails is not that and never will be that, and it was never meant to be that. It's bigger now than I ever dreamed it would be and I went through a phase of really hating that fact.

"It's cool to be in *Alternative Press* and it's cool to be in *Option* magazine; they think you're cool 'cause nobody's ever heard of you. It's comfortable, it's nice to have that kind of support from the truly alternative fans who I think do have a bit more integrity than the people who are spoon-fed MTV videos all day. However, if it happens that you do start to sell more records, whether you've done anything consciously to sell out or people just started to listen to you, there's nothing you can do to stop that. I could say, 'I'm never gonna make another video again, and I'm never gonna make an album, I'm gonna make an album of sheer noise, just to bum everybody out.' But that's not being any more true than if I sat down and said, 'I'm gonna write fifteen "Head Like a Hole's" so that I can be Eddie Vedder.'

"The price you pay is that the media that was aware

of you and the fan base that was there from the start, they turn their backs on you because you 'sold out.' Even though it's the *same* record they bought six months ago. And then it's not *cool* to like these guys if you're really *cool* because other people that aren't *cool* like 'em now. Bullshit. I felt really bad about it at first. I wished people would quit liking us and we could go back to play the *cool* club and, you know, stay in the *cool* magazines and worry about the *cool* people. Then I thought, '*Fuck the cool people. Do what you do.*' The cool people that are worth a shit are still gonna like you if they liked you for the right reasons in the first place. The ones that are trend hoppers, fuck them. It's not about the music for them anyway, it's more about the statement of 'Look how aware I am. I found a band that *nobody's* gonna wanna hear, and that makes me *cool.*'

"There's nothing wrong with getting your stuff across to more people. I didn't get into music to make a lot of money or to be this big. But now that it's kind of happened, I think, 'Well, okay, how can I take advantage of this position?' I'm thinking of the fuckin' kid in Nebraska in the cornfield that just heard about Nine Inch Nails and then bought the record. And it doesn't sound like the Pearl Jam record . . . It might open his eyes and maybe he'll think, 'This is really cool. I'll go buy a Ministry album. I'll go buy a Skinny Puppy record.' "

Still, Reznor staunchly resists the notion that NIN's success is responsible for bringing industrial music into mainstream prominence, simply because he doesn't consider NIN to be an industrial band. Additionally, he insists that NIN's melding of industrial aggression and pop melody isn't as revolutionary as some would give him credit for.

"There's a scene that has been flourishing for the past five years or more. Underground club-oriented danceable music has been labeled industrial due to the lack of coming up with a new name," he pointed out to *Axcess*. "What was originally called industrial music was about twenty years ago, Throbbing Gristle and Test Dept. We have very little to do with it other than there is noise in my music and there is noise in theirs. I'm working in the context of a pop song structure whereas those bands didn't. And because someone didn't come up with a new name that separates those two somewhat unrelated genres, it tends to irritate all the old-school fans waving their flags of alternativeness and obscurity. So, I'd say I've borrowed from certain styles and bands like that. Maybe I've made it more accessible. And maybe by making it more accessible it's less exclusive.

"I realize that I'm working within the parameters of the music business," Trent told *Request*. "If I didn't want to sell records I wouldn't be on a record label. But although I like bands like Test Dept. and Coil, less song-oriented bands, I'm fully aware that Nine Inch Nails works within the context of writing songs with choruses and hooks. That gives it a certain degree of commerciality, and I think that's a good platform to slip in some messages that are a bit subversive."

He acknowledges that Nine Inch Nails's technological image has probably kept many mainstream rock fans at bay. "I'll tell anyone who comes to see us that we use tape on stage, we use synthesizers, and most of it comes out of a computer," he says. "You'd be surprised, if you sat in on a Metallica session, how much of that comes out of a computer, but people don't want to know that. It's all just marketing."

Conversely, many hidebound synth-ravers seem to have a problem accepting NIN's stylistic eclecticism. "Of course those techno-computer guys hate me. You can't really dance to Nine Inch Nails, we don't play fast enough and I don't know what the music sounds like on ecstacy. Yeah, I believe in song structure. Yeah, I care about the melody.

"In the electronic world, most people have gone the techno kind of route, which I never was that interested in. I like some of the sounds of it. It didn't hold my attention: a whole genre based on one song."

As he told *Musician*, "It seems like the media demand everything be categorized and labeled to be understood. That became really apparent when we went to England. This guy comes in to do an interview and he's really pissed at me. What have I done? And he's fuming—'Well, what kind of music do you guys play? Are you electronic? Then why the guitars? And your show was bordering on being theatrical—what's going on?' I said, 'You're the one who's making up the names, I just do what I do. I'm sorry I don't fit into your retro-synthesizer-cyberpunkcategory bullshit.' I'm watching him struggle with, 'I want to like this . . . but I can't because I don't know what I'm liking.' If I told him it was electronic, he'd still be pissed off because it wasn't pure electronic—'Wait, you're a synth band but you use guitars!' Well, *blow me*."

CHAPTER 19

By now, Reznor, whose vampiric good looks have led *Playgirl* magazine to dub him one of the world's ten sexiest rockers, is not only a genuine superstar, but one for whom fans feel a genuine—and sometimes frightening—personal affinity, reflected in the often violent, out-of-control behavior of NIN concert crowds. It is now a regular occurence for Reznor to receive piles of deeply troubled poetry and personal diaries—not to mention sexual solicitations—from his admirers.

"I've always felt a little bit like a misfit," he mused to *Huh*. "I just don't belong. I don't know why. My life, I think, from the start has been a bit abnormal. I didn't have a family structure really. And . . . looking back it's always like there was *the club*. And I was like always *almost* in there. Never had much close friends or anything like that. Now I'm the *president* of the club. And they think they know me.

"Offstage, I'm always trying to be nice to everyone, trying not to be . . . let's say you really respect somebody, and finally you get a chance to talk with them and they're a dick. I'm so aware of that, and I overcompensate. I know what it's like to be a fan. But it's not really how I want to act, you know what I mean? I've just finished a fucking show. I don't care that you want to kill yourself. I'm sorry. Too bad. No, don't give me your poetry. And no, I don't want to go and do drugs.

"I don't know what kind of mail a mainstream rock band gets but we get about one letter out of a thousand that says, 'Your music is the only thing that keeps me going.' And then, 'I totally relate to what you're saying, however . . . ' Insert horrible situation: 'My parents beat me; I'm gonna run away; I'm a drug addict; I've tried to kill myself . . . and if you get this please just call me and respond . . . you don't know how much it would mean . . . that would keep me going.' I didn't know what to do. I could call this person up, but I'm inevitably going to let them down. I can't talk to you one hundred times a day. And if I write a little note, you get one back the next day and another the day after. . . . I felt shitty about this for four or five days, and after talking to some people I thought the best thing was not to, because I did exchange letters with a woman once and she wanted tickets and she showed up with this, 'Hi, we're engaged to be married' scenario.

"I try to make a point of not being a dick to anyone who comes up to me, and believe me there are many times when you don't want someone on your bus fucking with you. I always try to think about if I were meeting someone I respected . . . Prince was in the studio here the first day I came in, and somebody said, 'Hey, Prince likes your stuff, he had your *Broken* CD in the car.' . . . I thought they were kidding, 'cause this is a guy whose work I respect immensely. Figured it might just be cool to say hi if I ran into him around the studio. Then I find myself at one end of a big long hallway and he's at the other end walking toward me. So I simply said 'Hi' and waited for him to make eye contact. He just turned away. That strikes a wrong chord in my Midwestern upbringing regarding simple human decency. I don't mean to sound judgmental, but I've no great desire to meet Bowie now, because in my mind, I'd rather think of him as this cool guy."

He remains distinctly unimpressed by some of the less fulfilling by-products of mass success. "I like making music, I like touring, but I could do without the publicity side of things, and interviews and personality profiles, and people probing into my own life about whatever they think they need to know, or they think they know about me. The whole music as fashion thing, I try to stay away from it. But I kind of realize that it is a necessary part of an image and the way I'm portrayed is part of the whole ball of wax."

He was also dismayed to learn that "Closer," a song written as a deeply personal meditation on self-hatred, has been misinterpreted as an anthem of lust, thanks largely to its undeniably memorable chorus, "I want to fuck you like an animal." The song, he says, is "supernegative and superhateful. It's 'I am a piece of shit and I am declaring that and if you think you want me, here I am.' I didn't think it would become a frat-party anthem or a titty-dancer anthem.

"I got dragged into a strip club a few months ago," he told *Rolling Stone*. "To my absolute horror, I realized the DJ was playing 'Hurt,' a song based on the most personal sentiments, the deepest emotions I have ever had. We were crying when we made it, it was so intense. I didn't know if I even wanted to put it on the album. But there we were, and there it was, and girls were taking their clothes off to it."

Though Reznor has been embraced as an icon/role

model by a legion of tattooed, body-pierced admirers, he himself has no tattoos and his only pierced body parts are his ears. "I thought about getting branded, but I don't have the right kind of skin. I could lighten a dark room with the underside of my arms. I had my septum pierced for a year and a half, but when you're singing the mic hits, or your guitar strap pulls it when it goes over your head. Ouch."

URN HEAD LIKE A HOLE LER
E LIE-KINDA I WANT
OWN IN IT-HAPPINESS IN SLA
RY-SUCK- THE BECOMIN
ORT RING FINGER-SOMETHI
CAN NEVER HAVE-HELP ME I
HELL-MARCH OF THE PIGS
N-MR. SE
ESTRUCT-SANCTIFIED-THA
AT I GET- THE ONLY TIM
NION-WISH-LAST-GAVE
HROW THIS AWAY-REPTILIA
IGGY-HERESY-RUINER-I DO
ANT THIS-BIG MAN WITH
UN-A WARM PLACE-ERASE
EPTILE-DOWNWARD SPIRA
URN-HEAD LIKE A HOLE-TERI
E LIE-KINDA I WANT TO-DO
N IT-HAPPINESS IN SLAVER
UCK-THE BECOMING-HU
ING FINGER-SOMETHING I C
EVER HAVE-HELP ME I AM
ELL-MARCH OF THE PIGS-S
R SELF-DESTRUCT-SANCI
IED-THAT'S WHAT I GET-
NLY TIME-PINION-THE PIG
IN-MR. SELF DESTRUCT-SA

CHAPTER 20

An integral part of any relationship," Trent Reznor has said, "is knowing that you could be killed in your sleep at any time."

He admitted to *Details* that the violent, masochistic sex he's addressed in his songs and videos is a reflection of his own interests, "to a degree. I'm not a hard-core practitioner . . . Just the psychology behind it. I'm somewhat uncomfortable talking about this too much . . . "

When asked by *Details*'s Chris Heath if he'd ever kissed a man, he responded, "Yes, I've kissed a man. . . . A veil of drunkenness. It was kind of a mutual thing. It was weird. It was half joking around . . .

"In the old Nine Inch Nails, if we wanted to get rid of people, the guitar player and I would start making out. It was a trick. I mean, I really love women. I don't dislike men, and there's many times I've thought about it. You get into certain scenes, and I realize I should experiment down that path, and I just haven't done it yet. I've been in situations where there's men involved, but not directly interacting."

He went on to state that, for him, wild on-the-road sexual adventurism is "not a common situation. When I'm in a relationship that overpowers the desire to . . . these usually arise from casual situations. You wake up and think, 'Okay, we just stepped through another portal . . . ' I think about giving head, though. I'd be good at giving head, because I know what . . . I mean, no one knows how to jack yourself off better than yourself, you know?"

Reznor admits that the obsessive sense of control that allows him to stay sequestered in his studio for days on end springs in equal parts from his obsessive perfectionism and a desire to escape from the demands of the outside world. He cops to being a moody, controlling workaholic, devoting virtually every waking hour to work, to the detriment of personal relationships.

"I never allowed myself to really get in a totally serious relationship," he told *USA Today*. "For one thing, I was so poor I was ashamed of it . . . That's not a real reason. The real reason is I wanted to do what I'm doing and I didn't want anything to hold me back. When things started happening, every other element in my life was pushed to the back burner. I was excited by the work, but the price I paid was a sense of normality, a community of friends and a successful relationship."

Another unwanted by-product of Reznor's celebrity was a bizarre feud with Courtney Love, leader of Hole, widow of Kurt Cobain and all-around loose media cannon. Reznor and Love met when he heard that she was interested in playing with Nine Inch Nails, and he agreed to let Hole open six NIN shows in the autumn of 1994. "I thought, 'What's the worst that can happen?'," he later told *Details*. "Famous last words . . . "

They didn't speak for the first three shows. "In Cleveland she was completely intoxicated, a fucking mess," he told *Details*, adding that at one aftershow party, Love was passed out on a pool table with her dress hiked up, while onlookers snapped pictures. "I thought that was shitty. I'd be upset if people I thought cared about me allowed me to be in that position."

Before Reznor knew it, Love was badmouthing him and his band onstage, even though she was opening for NIN. "What I didn't know then was her fierce competitiveness when she's opening for somebody—she's carrying the weight of alternative credibility on her back, and we're a new-wave faggot band that's easily dismissed. Even though my crowd doesn't give a shit about that."

When the tour played Detroit, Reznor told *Details*, Love was having voice problems, and he offered to mix her one of the herbal concoctions that he uses in such situations. The two notoriously extreme personalities struck up a friendship—at least briefly.

"I thought she was really smart, which you couldn't tell from her behavior. But she was obsessed with media and how she's perceived. What I didn't realize was that 95 percent of it was her directly calling editors. She's got a full media network going on."

Their acquaintance soon began spawning vague yet vicious recriminations from Love. Despite Love's insistence to the contrary, Reznor maintains that the pair did not have a sexual relationship. According to Trent, "I think if there was an attraction on her part toward me, it was maybe because I showed compassion. The bottom line was, I thought I was around someone who was a victim and somebody who could use a friend, and what I was around was a very good manipulator and a careerist, someone not to be underestimated."

The feud quickly took on a progressively more nasty edge, with Love claiming that she'd had an affair with Trent and that he was a bad (and underendowed) lover. Rumors also spread that she was pregnant with his child. "It would be the second Immaculate Conception," Reznor responded.

Love further stated that Reznor didn't want to be seen publicly with her because it was bad for his image, and even stooped to accuse him of owning a silver Porsche.

"I thought (Trent) would have a lot of problems like Kurt, but that I could fix them," Love stated in an interview. During a concert in Holland, she taunted a female fan by asking, "Are you jealous of me because I slept with Trent Reznor?"

She also accused Reznor of being a misogynist and a homophobe. "I've never heard anyone that says faggot so much, this faggot, that faggot," she told a journalist. "Not a gay person in the entire organization. They hate gay people. Anyone that's gay that thinks Nine Inch Nails is like a sexually open band, Trent's lyrics are just stupid. I mean, dude, it's like if I played to an urban audience and called them niggers when I got off stage. He hates faggots."

It could be pointed out, however, that Love's attempts to paint Reznor as a homophobe are a bit hard to swallow in light of his forthrightness about his own sexual issues, not to mention his anecdotes of public makeout sessions with Rich Patrick. At one point, while working on *Broken*, in response to a homophobic comment made by a studio employee, Reznor bought a stack of gay porno magazines, clipped hundreds of photos of penises and hid them all over the studio, where they turned up for months afterward.

Love also painted the Nine Inch Nails entourage as a haven for groupies. "There's a real excess of that problem around that band and it's really disgusting where he thinks he's simply the largest recording star since Elvis Presley and all of his people do too."

She did manage to summon up some words of praise for Reznor's songwriting talents, albeit in a decidedly backhanded manner. "A lot of our lyrics are very similar, although mine are better. He's like Byron, it's obvious. I'm a lot more Shelley, or actually more like Yeats." After comparing Reznor unfavorably to her late exhusband and Smashing Pumpkins leader Billy Corgan, Love stated, "Trent, I think, has written three really great songs in his career, which is a hell of a lot more than you can say for most bands."

As the war of words escalated, rumors spread that Love was hounding Trent with a series of faxes and phone calls, before the pair abruptly buried the hatchet and called a truce. The surprise cease-fire reportedly led to a nationally distributed music magazine agreeing, at the last minute, to black out some Love-related Reznor quotes from a Nine Inch Nails feature, at the request of the NIN camp.

The one charge levelled by Courtney Love that

Reznor will cop to is his ownership of the aforementioned silver Porsche. "I had the money and I wanted a nice car to drive because it was fun, driving at five-hundred miles per hour wondering if it's going to flip over and kill me and I'll die a glamorous death. It isn't to take models to movie premieres in," Trent explained.

CHAPTER 21

Reznor recorded a mordant cover of Joy Division's "Dead Souls" for the soundtrack of the 1994 supernatural revenge drama *The Crow,* inspired by the cult comic book of the same name. The movie had made headlines even before its release, when star Brandon Lee—son of the late martial arts legend Bruce Lee—was killed in a freak shooting accident during filming. Considering *The Crow*'s macabre pedigree, Nine Inch Nails's involvement seemed only natural.

Reznor's next movie project—serving as musical director for controversial director Oliver Stone's much-discussed examination of America's fascination with serial murderers, *Natural Born Killers*—was considerably more challenging.

While the use of pop and rock songs in films is nothing new, *Natural Born Killers* took a riskier, more ambitious approach. Slaving over a makeshift recording/editing set-up in hotel rooms during his off-hours on the European leg of the Self-Destruct tour, Reznor assembled a diverse array of preexisting and newly recorded tracks into an evocative sonic pastiche that accompanied, and subtly commented on, the bloodthirsty exploits of the film's protagonists Mickey and Mallory, played by Woody Harrelson and Juliette Lewis.

It seemed appropriate that Stone—whose prior works *Platoon, The Doors* and *JFK* had touched on America's historical relationship with brutality—would tap Reznor, whose fascination with the darker corners of the human psyche made him a natural for the project.

While Reznor interpolated over eighty pieces of music into the film itself, the seventy-five-minute *Natural Born Killers* soundtrack album (the credits for which read "Produced, conceived and assembled by Trent Reznor") contains twenty-seven separate tracks, including old and new numbers by a startlingly diverse array of artists including Leonard Cohen, L7, Patti Smith, Cowboy Junkies, Bob Dylan, Duane Eddy, Patsy Cline, Nusrat Fateh Ali Khan, Jane's Addiction, Dr. Dre, Lard and the Dogg Pound. Many of those tracks were edited, extended and/or interspersed with snatches of dialogue from the film.

The assignment also called for Reznor to come up with a new Nine Inch Nails song, the seething, vengeful "Burn," which appeared on the soundtrack alongside two other NIN tunes, "A Warm Place" and an extended version of "Something I Can Never Have."

"Part of Oliver's deal with Warner Brothers," Reznor explained, "was that there had to be some new music on the soundtrack. So at one point he asked me to write a song for the movie. I agreed to try, but didn't think I could do it because I'd never written a song for anything. I was trying to get something thematically without calling it 'Natural Born Killers.' "

Thanks to Reznor's sensitive assembly of an intimidatingly diverse array of musical elements, the *Natural Born Killers* album is a remarkably cohesive listening experience, functioning equally well as an impressionistic retelling of the film's disturbing story and on its own merits as a sort of abstract mind-movie.

His *Natural Born Killers* experience left Reznor with a heightened interest in film work. "I'd like to do a real soundtrack," he said. "I'm interested in composing, whereas basically this was just editing. I made a little souvenir of the movie but I don't really feel I've created anything that, I would like to do—if we ever manage to stop touring."

Thanks to the publicity attached to recording at the Sharon Tate house, Reznor had already encountered more than his share of obsessive serial-killer buffs. "I'm not personally infatuated with serial killers," he said. "I find them mildly interesting at best, I have a curiosity about that, but by no means do I wish to glamorize them. From living in that house I've met every person in the world you can imagine who's obsessed with that whole thing and it's given me more of a perspective on it.

"We did this long-form video around *Broken* and a lot of people thought I'd become fascinated with serial killers, which I'm not. It's more about questioning my own motives—do I have it in me where I could do that? Like in *Silence of the Lambs* or *Red Dragon*, where the scariest thing is when the detective realizes that he has this side of his brain where he could figure out what the killer could be doing. Because he has part of that in him. Facing that. Not that I'd go out and kill somebody . . . "

In a cover story in the February 1996 issue of *Spin*, Reznor suggested that Nine Inch Nails's popularity might bear some relation to the perverse American obsession with violence that the movie explored. "If that didn't exist, we probably wouldn't exist," he said, but added, "but I don't think we're shock and carnage for shock and carnage's sake. I think there's more to Nine Inch Nails than looking at the wreck on the interstate. You want to turn your head and look, and hopefully see blood. There's an element of that fascination that has been worked into the imagery I've surrounded myself with, in music. It fascinates me, to a degree. I still watch *Cops*."

In a cover story in the September 8, 1994 issue of *Rolling Stone*, writer Jonathan Gold described the scene in the studio control room at Miami's South Beach Studios, where Reznor was putting the finishing touches on the *Natural Born Killers* soundtrack. While recording amidst a personally arranged array of candles and bound-and-gagged department-store mannequins, Reznor bemoaned the difficulty of keeping his computer programs straight when recording. "We try to name all our hard drives something easy to remember, like Bum Cleaver, Cunny or Big Hairy Pussy. Sometimes it gets complicated when we don't remember if the file we're looking for is Assfuck 25 on the Fuckfuck 12 drive or Fuckfuck 12 on the Assfuck 25 drive. And when we're talking to each other in the studio, wondering aloud whether running the Cunnykick file through the Fuckchop program on the Asslick disc would help us access the Turbocunt compression . . . it's really like speaking another language altogether."

CHAPTER 22

It's never been any secret that the other members of Nine Inch Nails's live lineups are fundamentally hired hands, charged with the task of bringing Trent Reznor's musical vision to life. Perhaps the most prominent of the numerous secondary Nails was Richard Patrick, the lanky guitarist who was Reznor's beer-spitting onstage foil during NIN's TVT/Lollapalooza years. He was also, according to most sources, Trent's closest friend and associate offstage as well.

Patrick (brother of actor Robert Patrick, who played the villainous killer cyborg in *Terminator 2*) exited Nine Inch Nails less than amicably prior to the recording of *The Downward Spiral*. He resurfaced in 1995 as half of the recording duo Filter, whose debut album *Short Bus* became one of the year's surprise successes.

Patrick's partner in Filter is another alumnus of the NIN organization, Brian Liesegang, a Chicago computer whiz who'd met Reznor during the Lollapalooza tour. "He was having troubles with his keyboard player and he said to me, 'Hey, do you want to play keyboards?' I had just finished college. I was a big fan of Nine Inch Nails, so naturally I said, 'Of course.'" Liesegang moved to New Orleans, where he moved in with Reznor and worked on samples and programming for *Broken*.

The seeds of Patrick and Liesegang's partnership were sown, ironically enough, at the funeral of Lollapalooza-era NIN drummer Jeff Ward, and on a subsequent car trip to Los Angeles, where they were to meet up with Reznor in preparation for the recording of *The*

Downward Spiral. The pair say that, during a stopover at the Grand Canyon, they had a near-mystical experience that convinced them that they needed to work together.

Patrick, who had first used the name Filter for a demo he'd recorded in Cleveland during his NIN days, and Liesegang recorded the bulk of *Short Bus* in the house the two rented in Cleveland, prior to actually signing their current deal with Warner Bros./Reprise. The pair insist that the label was unaware of their NIN connections when it became interested in signing them.

"We did that whole record at home with no contract," Liesegang told *Rolling Stone.* "No producer, no label people dropping by. We sent a tape in every once in a while. Before we got the record deal, we had never played a live show—ever."

Short Bus's hard-hitting blend of dense electronic noise, corrosive bursts of distorted guitar, austere vocals and strong sense of melody certainly puts Filter in the same stylistic ballpark as NIN. But Filter's emphasis is squarely on rockiest song structures, as confirmed by a tongue-in-cheek note included in *Short Bus's* packaging: "There is a certain subset of musicians who for reasons unknown adhere to the false premise that 'electronic' music or the tools involved imply a lack of creativity or inspired performance. Technology in the hands of creative, intelligent individuals is a tool for art, not a hindrance. Filter, being members of the current millennia, admit freely to the use of such devices."

Short Bus spawned an unlikely hit with "Hey Man,

Nice Shot," which was widely and incorrectly interpreted as referring to Kurt Cobain's suicide. The song was actually written prior to Cobain's death, and was inspired by a Pennsylvania politician who, after being caught engaging in corrupt activities, blew his brains out at a press conference.

Patrick insists that the song was not intended to celebrate, or make light of, suicide. " 'Hey Man, Nice Shot' is about a guy doing something drastic," he told *Alternative Press*. "I responded to that as some guy trying to make his life better, by making it worse. And trying to make everyone else alive through suicide . . . I saw him do something that took a lot of balls—granted, it was very wrong—I still think that if you tried something and it was a fucked-up way of dealing with it, hey man, nice shot. You took a shot at something. I'm not condoning his death, but like a kamikaze pilot, he had the balls to do something."

While Patrick and Liesegang obviously share some of their former employer's musical and lyrical interests, Filter's musical and lyrical approach is entirely its own. As one critic put it, "Reznor's music is an emotional roller-coaster, the harrowing sound of someone pulling out his own heartstrings by the roots, wanting you to hurt over it. Filter, on the other hand, comes more from the outside: just as harrowing, perhaps, but with more exploration of external causes and possibilities of a good solution—or at least some sort of a resolution."

The pair also share with Reznor a lack of interest in

being closely identified with the industrial genre. As Patrick said to *Rolling Stone*, "In 1987 there were two records that established industrial music, (Skinny Puppy's) *Vivisect* and (Ministry's) *The Land of Rape and Honey*. Ever since then, everything has been sucking off them like leeches."

Despite the two bands' musical common ground, Reznor's public comments about his former pals have been less than enthusiastic; he seems to regard the pair's defection as a personal betrayal. In an *Alternative Press* interview, for instance, he described Patrick as having "gone from being my best friend to somebody who hates my guts because somehow I stopped him from realizing his potential as a singer/songwriter."

Reznor had told *Spin* that his original plan for recording *The Downward Spiral* had called for Patrick to be an active studio participant, "but he wanted to be the guy that got recognized for writing the songs and singing. I didn't realize his real agenda was to have a way out of L.A. to get a record deal for himself."

In the same 1996 *Spin* feature, Trent further claimed that the only contact between himself and Patrick since the split had been "a drunken phone call (from Patrick) to say hello. And then asking an ex-girlfriend of mine out on a date. Those guys, in their minds, they're stars."

Despite Trent's recriminations, Patrick and Liesegang seemed to go out of their way to avoid bad-mouthing Reznor. "People wonder why we dodge Nine Inch Nails questions," Liesegang said to *Rolling Stone*, "and that's because we didn't have a whole fucking lot to do with it.

Nine Inch Nails was Trent's show. It's like thinking back to a high school buddy."

Patrick told the online music magazine *Addicted to Noise* that his departure from Nine Inch Nails was mainly a matter of feeling stifled by his limited role within the group. "I was the touring guitar player," he said. "If you like that, and you like touring, that's fine. If you don't, well, you've got some tough choices to make. I wasn't too sure whether I wanted to be twenty-six, twenty-seven, twenty-eight going on the road playing songs that I didn't have anything to do with. I just couldn't wake up and be twenty-seven and be a hired hand, playing guitar for the rest of my life in that band. I had that spirit in the beginning, but that kind of left.

"I had the easiest job in the world," Patrick told *Alternative Press*. "It was a fun childhood, but there was more to life after seven tours. 'Wow, I'm going to go out and spit beer on someone.' (My leaving) became a very natural solution to some of the things that were going on in my life. I was just happy to realize that I could send out a demo tape and get a deal.

"I hated the frustration involved in being in that band," Patrick continued. "Everybody (in NIN) seemed so unhappy and so pissed off. Angry at nothing. And I don't wanna live my life like that. I don't want to wake up every day and be angry. I want to enjoy life."

There was also apparently some tension over John Malm helping to set Patrick up with musical gear and studio time to work on his own material. Ultimately, though, according to Patrick, "It wasn't Trent, it wasn't John. It was me saying, 'I don't know if I can be a hired gun anymore.' I wanted to be creative, and Trent extended his hand and said 'Come on.' I'd be with him and we'd try to write. I'd look into his eyes and it was like, 'I don't know where you are going, I don't know what I want.' He knew it, I knew it and we said that we gotta try harder, but it wasn't gonna happen.

"It was a frustrating thing for me. I didn't know what I was mad at. I didn't know why it was hard for me to be in that band. I realized that it couldn't go on. I couldn't go on the road and be the guitar player that couldn't write what he plays. It was frustrating because I had to come to that realization. Even though Trent really did try to work it out with me, I couldn't even face him anymore. It was one of the most difficult times in my life."

Liesegang agreed that there simply wasn't room in NIN for any creative contributions he or Patrick could offer. "Nine Inch Nails is Trent's show. And it should be. He's great at working alone. He's tried working with other people and he's unhappy working that way. He doesn't *need* anyone else. As thinking, creative individuals, that was frustrating for us, and it was frustrating for him because it's not reconcilable."

Liesegang expresses regret over his and Patrick's strained relationship with their ex-boss. "Trent was someone I always looked up to, and I don't know him as well as Rich did. We lived in a house together in the middle of nowhere. My memories now, in hindsight, are positive. I think ultimately that Trent is very talented. He doesn't need anybody else and, for that reason, shouldn't be with anyone else. I think he tortures himself, but that's part of his craft. I just hope someday, and someday soon, there's a time where Rich, Trent and I can sit down and have a pitcher, and not talk about the business or talk about music, just talk the shit."

When discussing Reznor in interviews, Patrick and Liesegang paint a portrait of a sharply contradictory personality, equally capable of supportive kindness and bitter resentment. "Trent is probably one of the most . . . unhappiest human beings I've ever, ever, ever, ever known," stated Patrick. "And at times he was the meanest human being I've ever known. But there were *always* times where we would joke and joke and joke around for hours.

"He was always supportive, but we knew it couldn't happen within the confines of Nine Inch Nails. One time he was mixing tracks for *Downward Spiral* and he packed up his stuff to go work on the four-track in back of the house just so I could mix my own stuff. That's the Trent Reznor a lot of people don't know."

Both halves of Filter—which, like NIN, is augmented by additional players for live shows—seem genuinely appreciative of the lessons they'd learned from working with Reznor. "Trent taught me that two little notes like B and C sharp can be approached as 'Fuck you, Fuck you,' and that any guitar part, no matter how small, can convey attitude," said Patrick. "As long as you're playing with conviction, it's legitimate."

At the time that the Filter album had begun to establish Patrick and Liesegang as artists in their own right, they said that they hadn't spoken to Reznor in a year and a half. "It would be great," Patrick said wistfully, "to call him up and say, 'Let's go fishing, let's go to an arcade, let's go have a beer together' . . . "

CHAPTER 23

The end of 1994 brought a flood of honors and awards for Nine Inch Nails and *The Downward Spiral*. Trent Reznor was voted Artist of the Year by *Musician* and in *Spin*'s readers' poll, as well as being named one of *Entertainment Weekly*'s Top 10 entertainers of the year. "Closer" was voted Number One single by *Rolling Stone*'s readers. And NIN finished first in the Best Band, Best Album and Best Live Act stakes of *Alternative Press*'s year-end honors.

Additionally, *The Downward Spiral* was nominated for a Grammy as Best Alternative Album, up against discs by Green Day, Sarah McLachlan, Crash Test Dummies and Trent's pal Tori Amos. Retro-punk revivalists Green Day ended up taking the award home.

In May 1995, Interscope released another collection of remixed Nine Inch Nails numbers, *Further Down the Spiral*, with the new mixes handled by such Reznor pals as Rick Rubin, Jim "Foetus" Thirlwell, Coil, the Aphex Twin and longtime NIN live sound engineer Sean Beaven. Also credited on the disc were two additional musicians, Jane's Addiction/Red Hot Chili Peppers guitarist Dave Navarro and former Poco/Crosby, Stills and Nash keyboardist Kim Bullard, neither of whom had played on *The Downward Spiral*. As on the similar *Fixed*, *Further Down the Spiral* boasts several radical reworkings that cast the original songs in an entirely new light, while maintaining a good deal of the original album's spirit.

Further Down the Spiral was also released in a number of overseas variations that served to further confuse the band's already tangled international discography. While the domestic edition included eleven new mixes, fans in the U.K. got an alternate ten-track version—packaged in a cardboard sleeve rather than the U.S. release's jewel box—which included four tracks not on the domestic release, including versions of "Heresy" and "Ruiner" remixed by NIN's new live keyboardist, Charlie Clouser, and a live version of "Hurt" which was used in that song's video. To complicate matters further, the Japanese version duplicates the British track sequence but adds "Reptilian." (Charlie Clouser, incidentally, came to NIN with a résumé that already included production and/or remix work for the likes of White Zombie, Killing Joke, Prong, Die Krupps and Marilyn Manson.)

Meanwhile, Reznor found himself embroiled in a nasty new controversy. While NIN's knack for attracting controversy had thus far been useful in boosting the band's visibility, in 1995 this recurring phenomenon took on a simultaneously more serious and more absurd tinge, as Trent found himself dragged into a high-profile, right-wing media war on popular culture.

The latest round of trouble began when an unlikely alliance led by former U.S. Secretary of Education William Bennett and C. Delores Tucker, head of the National Political Congress of Black Women, began singling out Time Warner for releasing gangsta-rap records that they found objectionable, criticizing the corporation—which was hardly the only one releasing such music—for sanctioning those records' supposed endorsements of violence and misogyny. It wasn't long before Bennett and Tucker fixed their sights on Interscope, which was half-owned by Time Warner and whose roster included such prominent gangsta rappers as Dr. Dre, Snoop Doggy Dogg and the late Tupac Shakur.

The campaign took on a bizarre sense of theatricality when Bennett and Tucker showed up at the annual Time Warner shareholders' meeting in New York, and Tucker rose from the audience to launch a seventeen-minute diatribe against the company's supposed transgressions. In a private meeting with Time Warner executives that followed Tucker's soliloquy, Tucker challenged company officials to read the lyrics of Nine Inch Nails's "Big Man With a Gun" out loud; they declined. At one point, Tucker was reported to have referred to NIN as a gangsta-rap act.

Senate Majority leader and perennial Republican presidential hopeful Bob Dole soon hopped onto the bandwagon, also singling out Time Warner for its supposed crimes against the fragile minds of America's youth, rhetorically asking Time Warner execs, "Is this what you intended to accomplish with your careers? . . . You have sold your souls, but must you debase our nation and threaten our children as well?" In September, Time Warner caved in to its tormentors, selling off its 50 percent interest in Interscope to MCA.

Surprisingly, Reznor doesn't completely disagree with negative appraisals of "Big Man With a Gun." "The record was nearing completion," he explained to *Spin*. "I had written those lyrics pretty quickly and didn't know if I was going to use them or not. To me, *Downward Spiral* builds to a certain degree of madness, then it changes. That would be the last stage of delirium. So the original point of 'Big Man With a Gun' was madness. But it was also making fun of the whole misogynistic gangsta-rap bullshit. . . . From an artistic point of view, if I'd had a couple more months to look back on everything, I probably would not have put that song on the record. Just 'cause I don't think it's that good a song, not because I got spanked for it."

As for Tucker, Reznor commented, "She's such a fucking idiot," but added, "I think *The Downward Spiral* actually could be harmful, through implying and subliminally suggesting things, whereas a lot of the hardcore rap becomes cartoonish—it's real to youngsters, but it's so over the top."

Perhaps the last word on the issue should go to *Village Voice* critic Ann Powers, whose essay on "nasty art" took on the rising tide of pro-censorship sentiment of which the Time Warner/Interscope debacle seemed to be a symptom. Powers pointed out that, while many pundits had sprung to the defense of such more traditional underdogs like African-American rappers, Reznor and other artists "who don't play by clear political rules" hadn't received nearly as much support.

"Trent Reznor, who's now cultivating a whole set of Nine Inch Nails protégés on his own label, Nothing, just seems like a cartoon to most people over twenty-five, even though his music is a primary voice of resistance for his fans," Powers wrote. "The noise he makes, a complicated mix of lush melody and all-out ear abuse, gives shape to the rageful confusion that otherwise just sits in the stomachs of kids with no clear future and no reason to believe. Gangsta rap taps a similar anger . . . What all these artists share is a link to the Romantic-surrealist-dada-punk tradition of art as a bullet in the head of convention, one that, instead of killing, inflicts permanent brain damage."

By that time, though, Reznor didn't seem to care much what anybody thought of him. "I've come to the point where I don't give a shit, really. Everyone's like, 'Oh, Mr. Gloom' and all this. Fine. That's me but that's not all me. It's not really me. It's just who you want me to be. So here I am. Project me to be the biggest fucking cunt in the world. It's fine with me."

Ironically, while conservative groups were attacking Nine Inch Nails with increasing frequency and ferocity, Reznor's work was winning respect in some "serious" quarters. For example, the Mark Romanek-directed "Closer" video received an Association of Independent Commercial Producers' award for cinematic achievement, at a dignified black-tie affair at New York's Museum of Modern Art, where the video was added to MOMA's permanent archives.

CHAPTER 24

One of the artists who'd played a profound role in shaping Trent Reznor's musical consciousness was David Bowie, who in the seventies had brought the avant-garde into the mainstream, redefining the concept of the modern rock star. In short, Bowie was an alternative rock artist long before such a term existed.

Bowie's influential trilogy of late-seventies albums *Low*, *Heroes* and *Lodger* had been an inspiration to Reznor in the making of *The Downward Spiral*. Reznor even sampled a vocal line from "Time," from Bowie's 1973 album *Aladdin Sane*, on the *Further Down the Spiral* remix "Self-Destruction, Part Two."

So it must have been flattering for Reznor when Bowie invited Nine Inch Nails to sign on as opening act on his Fall 1995 *Outside* tour. Unfortunately, the reality of the situation was a bit less romantic. Bowie had grown musically adrift and commercially marginal in the eighties, and by the mid-nineties Bowie's career was distinctly moribund.

Though Bowie had, in his prime, been one of rock's most ingenious and inventive stylistic provocateurs, many observers viewed the Bowie/NIN pairing (and Bowie calling on Reznor to do a remix of the album's first single, "The Heart's Filthy Lesson") as a transparent attempt by the forty-eight-year-old former trendsetter to buy back some of his faded credibility by latching onto Reznor's cutting-edge bandwagon.

Indeed, tapping Nine Inch Nails as support act was a savvy move on Bowie's part, not only increasing the arena tour's drawing power but giving a shot in the arm to Bowie's faded hipness quotient, since the younger fans that comprised the core of NIN's audience would be more likely to remember Bowie as suave eighties lounge lizard than seventies innovator.

The tour—Bowie's first in five years and his first as a solo artist in eight—was in conjunction with the release of Bowie's 1995 album *Outside,* a vaguely conceptual work that reunited him with his late-seventies collaborator Brian Eno, and which was largely dismissed as a self-conscious bid to regain Bowie's credibility as a serious artiste. The English daily *The Independent,* for instance, opined that "*Outside* sounds like fodder for an industrial-music Broadway show based on *Blade Runner*" and characterized the live pairing with NIN as "a patently calculated Bowie move."

Though Bowie was the nominal headliner (with NIN/Nothing Records protégés Prick opening the shows), the former Thin White Duke's faded commercial status—not to mention the relatively mediocre quality of his new material—resulted in NIN stealing much of his musical thunder. The fact that the live Nails had matured into a lean, mean performing machine didn't hurt either, and many sated NIN fans—possibly worn out from slugging it out in the mosh pit that had been provided for the occasion—left before or during Bowie's set.

As *Rolling Stone*'s Al Weisel observed, "The introspective studio wunderkind who once stalked the stage like a caged animal has evolved into a confident band leader, taking NIN through a relentless, exhilirating survey of his career. The group has been reimagined as a stripped-down postpunk ensemble, supplanting drum machines with two drummers and de-emphasizing synthesizers for guitars."

Reviewing the show at Los Angeles' Forum, *Variety* reviewer Phil Gallo reported, "Nine Inch Nails supplied the first forty minutes of this combo effort, artfully cresting and plummeting on the dynamic range with soft acoustic interludes and throbbing industrial mayhem. NIN has ordered chaos with clever precision, much as Bowie did all those years ago in the guises of Ziggy Stardust, Aladdin Sane and the Thin White Duke. In this era of primal scream-driven emotional honesty within every genre, Reznor scrapes the recesses of his subconscious and lays it on the table for examination that, despite the lack of intimacy in a hall like the Forum, manages to work."

Rather than playing separate sets, the Bowie and NIN portions of the show were interwoven. The end of NIN's set segued into the beginning of Bowie's, with Bowie and Reznor sharing the stage for five songs and about thirty minutes. The *Downward Spiral* number "Eraser" eased into Bowie's "Subteranneans," with Reznor playing sax and the remaining Nails providing backup, after which Reznor moved to keyboards and shared vocals with Bowie on an industrialized rearrangement of Bowie's "Scary Monsters." The two frontmen traded vocals on the NIN tune "Reptile," with Reznor's raw, emotional squall providing a neat counterpoint for Bowie's smooth, theatrical croon.

The new Bowie number "Hallo Spaceboy" found Bowie and Reznor performing with both bands—with NIN clad in their traditional black and Bowie's sidemen dressed in white—sharing the stage, before Bowie's musicians took over for Bowie's smoothed-out reworking of Reznor's "Hurt."

Though Reznor seemed pleased to be working with his idol, critics were divided over the appropriateness of the pairing. *New York Times* critic Jon Pareles stated, "While Bowie and Reznor are kindred performers in some ways, they are polar opposites in others. Reznor is an explosive introvert, ranting and agonizing over his private torments while Nine Inch Nails hammers blunt, primal riffs. It's clear what's on his mind. Bowie, by contrast, is a detached observer, parceling out disconnected hints and images, moving in and out of the stories he suggests. His songs are more abstract, even at their most impassioned."

Boston Globe critic Jim Sullivan pointed out, "Bowie and Reznor . . . share an approach that considers rock as art, and art as a challenge (and) a writerly, if creepy, interest in mayhem and murder . . . Bowie and Reznor also unflinchingly embrace a chaotic world (where) order is impossible, logic flawed, violence prevalent. They both relish texture, arrangements that break with convention. And they're both eager to take a risk in a sometimes staid rock culture. . . . Reznor is confrontational, in-your-face; Bowie is more about subtext. You might say Reznor has an attitude problem and Bowie has an attitudinal pose."

To his credit, Bowie didn't take the easy way out, performing few of his well-known hits and concentrating instead on more challenging, older material, and many songs from the oblique, not-yet-released *Outside*. Still, it was generally agreed that Nine Inch Nails—whose visceral wallop easily overshadowed Bowie's stripped-down, non-theatrical presentation—was the hands-down winner in this high-profile battle of the bands.

According to the *Times*'s Pareles, "Reznor captures adolescent terror and confusion with terse clarity. Sex is feared and desired; authority is reviled; loneliness, distrust, pent-up rage, self-hatred and self-aggrandizement all churn together. His songs have percussive brute force—many started with drumbeats alone—and muscular finesse, shifting from a metallic guitar attack to the swooping, cutting keyboards of dance music." On balance, Pareles concluded, "Reznor's avenging misery was an easier concept to grasp than Bowie's millennial malaise."

Many of the tour's notices were like that of the *Boston Herald*, which observed, "The Man Who Fell to Earth fell flat on his face Saturday night" and called the co-bill "the upstaging of a lifetime."

Ever the trouper, Bowie seemed to take the situation in stride. "They're there decidedly to see the Nails," he said of the NIN fans who comprised the bulk of the tour's crowds. "I think most of them haven't a clue what I do. In fact, when I do 'The Man Who Sold the World,' I think they think it's really cool that I covered Nirvana.

"I'm playing to a hardcore Nails fan between the

ages of fourteen and twenty-two," Bowie commented to the New York *Daily News.* "They can often be found doing something called body-surfing during my version of Jacques Brel's 'My Death.'

"I slip onstage after a set by the most aggressive band ever to enter the Top Five," he further reasoned. "I do not do hits. I perform lots of songs from an album that hasn't even been released. The older songs I perform are probably obscure even to my oldest fans. I use no theatrics, no videos and offer no costumes. It's a dirty job. And I think I'm just the man for it."

Reznor, meanwhile, seemed to be enjoying himself, though he later admitted to being intimidated by Bowie's presence. "I found myself kind of hoping that he wouldn't be sitting there, so I wouldn't have to talk to him. Not that I didn't like him. But I felt like I had to impress him. I had to impress his band. I couldn't just let my hair down."

Still, he added that Bowie's musicians "hung out in our dressing room all the time. They didn't want to sit around reading poetry and talking about fucking German art movies. They wanted to hang out."

CHAPTER 25

Nine Inch Nails followed the Bowie dates with a short series of low-key club gigs in the southern U.S. Those shows, like several on the Bowie tour, were recorded for a possible live album and/or video, with director Simon Maxwell (who had shot the band's live performance-based video for "Hurt") handling camera duties. The video was originally intended for release in time for Christmas 1996, but the project was shelved, reportedly because Reznor was unhappy with the film footage.

The live video was intended to be the first NIN project to be completed at Reznor's recently completed New Orleans studio complex. The complex included a customized recording facility along with Trent's collection of vintage video arcade games, a classic Kiss pinball machine and the torture chair featured in the "Happiness In Slavery" video. It was at the studio that Reznor, a big fan of the video game Doom, composed and recorded the music for its sequel, Quake.

In addition to the studio, Reznor had purchased a beautiful two-story Southern manse located on a quiet street in the city's Garden District. Trent's status as a Crescent City celebrity was confirmed when a local newspaper ran a photo of the house and printed its location on the front page of its Sunday edition.

Nothing Records kicked off 1997 with the release of the Reznor-assembled soundtrack album of *Lost Highway*, a film-noir excursion directed by *Eraserhead/Blue Velvet/Twin Peaks* director David Lynch, whose fascination with the seamy underside of everyday life makes him a fascinating match for Trent. In addition to the jittery new Nine Inch Nails track "The Perfect Drug" and two instrumental pieces credited to Trent Reznor rather than NIN, the album included material by longtime Lynch associate Angelo Badalamenti (who wrote the film's evocatively creepy score), Marilyn Manson, David Bowie, Lou Reed, Barry Adamson and the Smashing Pumpkins.

Speaking of the Smashing Pumpkins, Chris Vrenna was spotted drumming with that band during its performance on the Grammy Awards show in February 1997. His appearance with the Pumpkins—sharing the stage with another drummer, Matt Walker, who, ironically had previously played with ex-NINsters Rich Patrick and Brian Liesegang in Filter—bolstered widespread speculation that Vrenna had once again exited the Nine Inch Nails camp.

As for the next Nine Inch Nails album, work on which was put on hold for the Bowie tour, Reznor told *RIP* in late 1994, "I just feel, like, a burst of creativity that I wanna make a record that's going to be opposite of *Downward Spiral.*" He added that he'd been considering involving the other members of the live band in the record, expressing the desire to make the next NIN album in a manner that's "not as isolating and perhaps a lot more collaborative."

He further stated that he'd "started coming up with sets of rules to work with it. I've got about four different little game plans, I'm gonna try to find out which one makes the most sense. I need to do that. And then I write within those guidelines. Which might sound silly, but . . .

"This time, I'm in the process of formulating how I want to approach this. Whether it might be a complete collaborative thing with three other people, or it might be getting rhythm ideas from different people and then constructing them into something and then farming it out to somebody else, while I'm not involved, see what comes back. Right now, if you ask me this second, I'm more into the idea of collaborating." But he cautioned against taking any of his speculation for granted. "You never know, I'm a moody guy."

In September 1996, while NIN fans continued to wonder what Trent's next move would be, the band made an unexpected one-off live appearance at New York's Irving Plaza, closing an evening of Nothing Records acts during the CMJ college radio music industry convention. Despite the excitement attached to NIN's appearance, the band was nearly upstaged by Marilyn Manson who, after a few songs, abruptly ended their set when drummer Ginger Fish was hit by a flying mic stand thrown by Mr. Manson and/or a bass guitar flung by bandmate Twiggy Ramirez.

Though his career prospects seem limitless, Reznor continues to balance the bright potential of his future with the personal demons that continue to drive his work. "I still don't know who the fuck I am," he said recently. "I know what I don't believe in. I know what I've rejected. But I'm not sure yet what I do believe in.

"Generally, I've always aspired to become part of something," he commented to Spin. "But I just never felt like it—it hasn't really happened. It's odd, because I have my big club now, and I'm president. It's not like I'm a part of it though. When I went to college, I thought that all I wanted to do was just disappear and see what it's like to have friends, be in a group. Two months later, I was like, fuck this. I'm not like you. I don't want to lose my identity, my independence, by being around a bunch of other people who are also scared, doing the same thing. Hiding behind something printed on a T-shirt that gives you a sense of who you are.

"When I go into an interview on MTV I don't kick into the David Lee Roth joke-around-be-a-rock-fuckhead mode like they want you to be. When you're on tour, you're expected to act a certain way and you're encouraged to act a certain way and when you don't, they don't know what to do with you. It just makes me feel like a fucking misfit because, okay, I didn't fit into anything my whole life and now I'm doing this thing and I don't fit into *that* either.

"I don't know how to do what I want, and I feel crushed because I have this shitty education. There's a lot of things I wish I knew about, like Eastern religions . . . I know what I *don't* believe in. I don't have my own life together really. I don't wake up in the morning feeling spiritually whole, or great about nature or God or the universe. And I've been on a quest, instead of finding a way to start a life."

He also suggests that his days as a rock star may be numbered, and that his longterm musical future may lie in his desire to work behind the scenes, producing other artists. "There's going to be a point where I can't do both things," he says. "I can't do it. I tried. So at some point I would like to focus on production, which I would really like to do more of, but Nine Inch Nails eats up every second of my life."

Whatever his future holds, it seems a safe bet that Trent Reznor has a ways to go before resting.

"I'd like to bow out thinking, hey, I did that. I tried that. I experienced that. I wasn't afraid. Rather than sit in the back room with a fucking towel over my head, I want to be around it, absorb, consume."